The Worker in America

Jane Claypool

THE WORKER IN AMERICA

Issues in American History

Franklin Watts
New York/London/Toronto
Sydney/1985

For Sondra Herrera
with heartfelt thanks
for all her support
all these years.

Photographs courtesy of:
Culver Pictures, Inc.: pp. 10, 30, 84;
The Bettmann Archive: pp. 19, 63;
New York Public Library Picture Collection: p. 43;
Denver Public Library Western Collection: p. 46;
UPI/Bettmann Archive: pp. 91, 101;
AP/Wide World: p. 108.

Library of Congress Cataloging in Publication Data

Miner, Jane Claypool.
The worker in America.

(Issues in American history)
Includes index.
Summary: Examines the history of the American worker,
including the history of working blacks, women, and
immigrants, and discusses the development of labor unions
and work in the future.
1. Labor and laboring classes—United States—History—
Juvenile literature. [1. Labor and laboring classes—
History] I. Title. II. Series.
HD8066.M56 1985   331'.0973   84-27152
ISBN 0-531-04933-7

Contents

Introduction 1

Chapter 1
The Colonial Period
3

Chapter 2
Industrialization and Expansion
14

Chapter 3
The Growth of Unions
24

Chapter 4
Black Workers
37

Chapter 5
Immigrants Seek Opportunity
57

Chapter 6
Women in the Work Force
77

Chapter 7
The Worker in Postwar America
96

Chapter 8
Working in the Future
107

Index 117

Introduction

"America is the land of labor," Benjamin Franklin said, and it is true that America was settled primarily by workers–men and women who existed by means of their own labor instead of depending on inherited wealth or the work of others. These working people were eager to improve their living standard, and most chose to come to this country because it offered opportunities to get ahead economically to those who worked hard and saved their money.

Some were skilled workers who specialized in a particular craft. Others were unskilled laborers who had nothing to sell but their physical strength and willingness to sweat. Whether skilled or unskilled, workers were welcome here. From the time the Europeans first began to settle the continent, a chronic labor shortage provided many opportunities. New settlers could always find work cultivating the earth, building homes, fishing, or working as carpenters, tinsmiths, brickmakers, or other skilled craftsmen.

Nor was it just in colonial times that America attracted the willing worker. Immigration continues to this day, giving the United States one of the world's most diverse populations. Its citizens come from every cultural and racial group in the world, and these immigrants have helped to build a unique democracy based on common values. One of the most central beliefs in American society is in the value of hard work and the right of human beings to seek opportunities for advancement.

History books concentrate on famous leaders and events, but the history of the United States is not just the story of politicians, heroes, and wealthy leaders. It is also a history of ordinary men and women who worked with their hands to build the nation. This book attempts to give a wide view of the American worker's past and future. The first two chapters trace the early history of the nation and its workers; the third chapter explains the development of labor unions. Next, there are chapters on the working history of blacks, women, and immigrant groups, whose labor has contributed in special ways to building America. The book ends with a discussion of recent history and the future of the American worker.

1

The Colonial Period

The Native Americans

The first people on this continent depended directly on the land for their livelihood. Because the Native American population was small in relation to the amount of land they inhabited, most were hunters but many also farmed.

Over half of all the agricultural goods produced in the world today were discovered and cultivated by the Indians. Their foods included corn, tomatoes, white and sweet potatoes, and many kinds of beans as well as peanuts, pumpkins, and turkeys. In fact, none of the settlers who came to America from Europe ever discovered a wild plant or tree that the Indians did not know about and use.

The work the Indians developed were directly related to the materials of the earth. They manufactured homes from branches and animal skins, clothes from skins and plants, baskets from reeds, jugs from clay, and cooking pots from gourds or shells.

The Explorers

Although the lure of cheap or free land would bring the majority of the European settlers to America, the first ones who came to this continent were looking for riches. They were not settlers but adventurers who hoped to return to Europe as wealthy men. Once in the New World, however, some of these adventurers gave up their old occupations as soldiers and sailors and settled in the new land. Hernando Cortez, for instance, led the military campaign against the Aztec Indians and conquered the land that is now Mexico. Later, he became the Marqués del Valle, ruling much of southern Mexico.

The Haciendas of the Southwest
Cortez was one of the first major landholders in a system of government that was very much like the old serf system of the Middle Ages in Europe. Instead of castles, however, the people clustered around large houses called haciendas. Only the very richest people owned land under the hacienda system of the Southwest and California. The position of the workers was similar to that of the slaves and indentured servants who came to the Southeast; it was almost impossible to acquire land unless you were born to the ruling classes.

The workers who lived on the haciendas were Indians or people with a mixture of European and Indian blood. They worked as cattle tenders, sheep herders, servants, and farmers. The hacienda was basically self-sufficient, and the profits from the little trading done were used to buy luxuries for the owner or tools for the hacienda. For the most part, the hacienda workers lived directly from the lands they worked, eating the crops and meat they raised, wearing the cloth they wove, and using tools made from local materials. These workers built their houses of sun-dried adobe bricks and often had to carry water long distances in order to survive. Later, they dug irrigation ditches and built roads—heavy and difficult labor, especially with their simple tools.

Workers were often skilled at one or two particular occupations: tanning leather, braiding rope, shoeing horses, building carriages, metalsmithing, carpentry, or building adobe bricks. When the California missions were built, many Indians lived and worked on them, tending the vineyards and gardens. The most highly skilled carpenters and artisans decorated the mission churches and the homes of wealthy landowners.

The English Colonies
The first settlers on the eastern coast of North America were also looking for gold when they landed in Jamestown, Virginia, in 1607. The English were eager to catch up with the Spanish colonists, and the leader of that first colonial expedition, John Smith, had orders to find gold. He soon saw that the wealth of the land in Virginia would come from hard work rather than unearned treasure. He wrote back to England saying the authorities should send him "carpenters, husbandmen, gardeners, fishermen, blacksmiths, masons, diggers of trees' roots." He added that there was no gold and that "Nothing is to be expected thence but by labor."

But if the first colonists had hoped for gold, the ones who followed had more realistic expectations. Some colonists came to the new land for religious reasons; but most were lured by the promise of owning their own property. A chance to acquire land of one's own was a chance at becoming wealthy. Since colonial land had not been farmed in European fashion, the settlers thought of it as unowned and free for the taking. They pushed the Indians westward and established new colonies.

The Agricultural Life
Nearly all of the American colonists were farmers. In the South, the development of crops such as tobacco and later cotton, which were sold for export, led to the development of the plantation system. The southern plantation system of farming was similar to the Span-

ish hacienda system on the other side of the continent. The farms were large, and one owner had almost absolute authority over many workers.

Bound Labor

About 80 percent of the colonial labor force was made up of bound laborers—people who, to one degree or another, were owned by others for whom they were required to work. Black slaves and white indentured servants both fell in this category.

The first blacks who came to Virginia in 1619 were treated the same as white bound servants of that time— that is, they were freed after a period of years. By the 1640s, however, the practice of selling blacks into permanent slavery was common. Twenty years later, slavery had become an institution in the southern colonies and had the support of colonial laws. Indentured servants were white men and women who agreed to serve a period of bound labor in return for the opportunity to gain passage to America. They usually bound themselves as servants for four to seven years. At the end of that time they would be free to pursue their own lives in the New World.

By the end of the seventeenth century, England was shipping convicts to the colonies as bound servants instead of imprisoning them. Lesser crimes brought seven-year terms, and crimes punishable by death called for fourteen years of servitude. One court in London sent ten thousand convicts to America between 1717 and 1775. This practice was encouraged by some employers who found prison laborers less expensive than slaves or indentured servants, but it was criticized by many leaders. Benjamin Franklin protested that the British practice of "emptying their jails into our settlements is an insult and contempt, the cruellest that ever one people offered to another."

Bound labor also served as punishment for colonial debtors who would have been jailed if they had lived in England. In America, people were bound to their creditors to labor for a period of time until their debts were satisfied. Because of the chronic labor shortage, this system was considered a practical and humane way to satisfy a debt.

Free and Independent
No matter how difficult the term of servitude, once they completed their term the bound workers were free. Most chose to farm their own land, and they formed a class of farmers known as "poor whites," who owned small holdings and few or no slaves.

Although some large southern plantations supported as many as five hundred people, most southern colonists lived on small farms like those in the middle and northern states. The farmer, his family, and a few hired hands or slaves worked the land and raised their own food. Sometimes they also produced a surplus crop, which they sold to bring in extra income. In the South that cash crop was usually tobacco or cotton. Farther north, the crop might be squash, peas, barley, rye, corn, or pumpkins. Some small farmers also kept hogs and sheep, and those in the middle states could sell lumber and animal pelts as well as fruits and wheat. In the North, there was abundant fishing, too, and the maple trees yielded sugar.

All over the colonies, farm families strove for self-sufficiency. They wore homemade clothing and ate home-grown products. Most farmers were skilled at carpentry, simple mechanics, and other trades. They made their own furniture, barrels, boxes, and tools. Often they also made their own nails, shod their own horses, and split wood for shingles in their spare time.

Small farmers worked extremely hard, and some resented the comparative ease that the plantation owners enjoyed while slaves worked the fields. Most plantation owners came from the wealthy class and seldom worked with their hands, though some—like Thomas Jefferson and George Washington—had a real interest in and a scientific knowledge of agriculture.

Up north, especially in New England, the farms were tough to work. Farmers endured starvation and backbreaking work to make ends meet. The typical farmer worked alone, with one hired hand, or perhaps with his older children. A large family was considered a blessing in those days, because it meant there would be more people to work the land. Ten children were common in colonial families.

Children were put to work as soon as they were able. Even the four-year-olds were expected to do simple chores such as collecting eggs and sweeping floors. Boys of ten and older worked in the fields with their fathers each day. Grown sons were usually expected to live and work at home until they married. If the farm was large enough, the sons might live at home with their own families all their lives.

On smaller holdings, however, the question of who would live and work on the family farm after the children reached adulthood was often a difficult one. A large farm could be divided into several parcels, giving each child an equal inheritance, but most northern farms were too small to be divided so many times.

Sometimes the oldest son inherited the farm, and the other children had to fend for themselves. Other sons might head west and find virgin land of their own. Some went into trades or other occupations.

Daughters sometimes inherited all or part of a farm, but most were expected to marry and live on their husbands' land. An unmarried woman could own property in the colonies, and many did, but most lived on the family farm all of their lives and never owned any of it. Many daughters who did not marry were expected to care for their parents and, later, for the families of the brother who inherited the farm.

The New England
Merchants and Sailors
Because farming was so difficult in the rocky soil of the Northeast, some New Englanders turned to the sea for their livelihood. Fishing became a lucrative occupation, and many farm boys chose the life of a sailor.

Primarily because of the whaling industry, shipbuilding became an important occupation for carpenters and other tradesmen. New England harbors sang with the sounds of hammers and saws as American ships were launched, each one bigger, faster, and better than the last. The early American ships were small and clumsy by European standards, but the clipper ships of early 1800s were the most beautiful ever built. Fishing, shipbuilding, and merchant sailing remained important occupations in New England and the Middle Atlantic states until recent times.

Fish had been an important food from the beginning. As early as 1629, Francis Higginson of the Massachusetts Colony wrote, "The aboundance of SeaFish are almost beyond beleeuing." Bass, cod, mackerel, and lobster made some New England merchants wealthy, and there were also great quantitites of herring, turbot,

This eighteenth-century print shows several
aspects of the cod fishing industry in Colonial
America. At left is a man outfitted in the
clothing typical of a cod fisherman, holding
the line used in the industry. Other parts
of the picture show the fishing technique, and
the methods of salting and of drying the cod.

sturgeon, haddock, mullet, eels, crabs, mussels, and oysters. By the end of the seventeenth century, codfish was as basic to the Massachusetts economy as tobacco was to that of Virginia. In 1784 the Massachusetts legislature passed a resolution "to hang a representation of a Codfish in the room where the House sit, as a memorial to the importance of Cod-Fishery to the welfare of the Commonwealth."

In colonial times and shortly after, American merchant ships sailed all over the world, trading goods and making huge profits. The New England sea captains went to China, India, Portugal, and every land in between, trading beads, knives, gunpowder, and cotton goods for silks, spices, and furs. Sometimes the long voyages were very profitable. For instance, one captain bought from the Indians of the Northwest 560 otter skins in exchange for goods that had cost him only $2.00. He then sold the skins in Canton, China, for $22,400.

The goods the merchants brought back stimulated trade, and many New Englanders chose trading as an occupation instead of farming or sailing. Some became shopkeepers or peddlers as the retailing trade flourished in New England cities.

Several men amassed great fortunes in New England, and the independent spirit of these merchants, sailors, and craftsmen was one of the underlying causes of the American Revolution. Indeed, Boston's Faneuil Hall, the first gathering place of American rebels, was built by a merchant who had made his fortune carrying codfish to distant markets.

The Craftsmen
By the end of the colonial period, workers throughout the colonies were looking for more specialized ways to

earn a living. Many left agriculture because farms grew smaller as the colonies grew older. Some colonists pushed west; many others became skilled craftsmen in the small towns and cities that were springing up all over the continent.

Craftsmen learned trades by becoming apprentices to carpenters, printers, cabinetmakers, shoemakers, bakers, or silversmiths. These apprentices worked for three to seven years in return for their training, board, and room. Eventually the apprentice became a journeyman and earned a wage. By the time he was around the age of thirty, if he was good enough, he might become a master and set up his own business.

Most labor during the colonial period was custom work; that is, each product was made to order for a particular customer. Most items were made in the home of the craftsman, and all pieces were designed individually. Though the tools were simple, the craftsmanship of this period was exquisite. Examples of fine furniture and other crafts can be seen in museums today. Paul Revere, the famous revolutionary patriot, was one of the most gifted silversmiths of the period.

Colonial Prosperity
Throughout the colonial period there was a shortage of labor, and most immigrants were able to find work immediately. A healthy colonist who worked hard could succeed, and ambitious men and women labored from dawn to sundown, saving their money and taking advantage of their opportunities in the hope of building a fortune for their families. Their success attracted other immigrants who labored just as hard. By the time of the Revolution, the new United States was a bustling, optimistic place filled with enthusiastic workers.

The American Revolution

In 1776, the people of the United States revolted against English rule. The same thirst for freedom and equal opportunity that attracted earlier colonists led them to fight for their independence from the British.

Most of the leaders of the Revolution were members of the wealthier class, but the ranks of the Continental Army were filled with carpenters, forgemen, smiths, wagoners, and other craftsmen. The workers gained much from the Revolution, including a chance to buy confiscated lands of British loyalists for low prices.

When the Constitution was ratified, workers turned out in large numbers to celebrate the event. In New York City on July 23, 1788, there was a large ratification parade in which six thousand workers from over fifty crafts marched. Heading a section of the parade marched a hundred bakers carrying "the federal loaf, ten feet long, twenty-seven inches in breadth, and eight inches in height." Representatives of other crafts included the butchers and the candlestickmakers.

In the next decade the factory system took hold, and the trade union movement began. By 1800, one out of six working Americans was employed in a pursuit other than agriculture. In the years that followed, American workers gained political and economic power to a degree undreamed of in Europe.

2 | Industrialization and Expansion

The Revolution was only the first of a series of dramatic changes for the American worker. At the beginning of the nineteenth century, the North, the South, and the West were all somewhat alike, but the differences between regions became dramatically pronounced as the Northeast entered a period of radical change referred to as the Industrial Revolution.

The Industrial Revolution

During the 150 years between 1812 and 1962, the United States was transformed from an agrarian society, in which 95 percent of the people worked on the land, into a modern industrial nation where only 5 percent of the workers were employed on farms.

The Industrial Revolution began in England in the 1700s, when a series of inventions led to the development of large power-driven machines and large factories which were common in England long before they were introduced to the United States.

The Industrialization of America

In 1800, about 60 percent of America's non–farm workers were skilled craftspeople. These workers were usually called mechanics, no matter what their specialty was. They owned their own tools and worked independently or in small shops. Some owned their own homes, and many had apprentices and servants working for them. These shopowners were masters, and those who worked for them for wages were journeymen. While they worked at specialized trades, they often cultivated their own gardens and kept a few farm animals as well. Some even practiced a second occupation. George Washington, for instance, ordered his shoes from a carpenter who cobbled on rainy days.

Journeymen labored long hours for low wages, and apprentices worked without any pay at all, but these craftsmen took great pride in their work. They helped to create fine products, many of which were individually signed or stamped. They also looked forward to the day when they would have their own shops. The standard of living of these skilled workers was higher than that of workers anywhere else in the world at that time, and they enjoyed the respect of the community.

About 40 percent of the urban working class consisted of unskilled workers. They did not live as well as the trained craftsmen. These unskilled laborers dug canals, loaded goods from ships, and did other work that required no training. Their wages (about a dollar a day in 1800) purchased only minimal food and shelter, and many of these workers were very poor.

Over a period of sixty years from 1812 until 1872, the Industrial Revolution changed the way nearly all goods were manufactured in the United States, and, in doing so, it changed the way people lived and worked. Manufacturing became a factory process, and the skilled craftsmen were no longer needed to produce a finished product.

New Production Techniques
Like the earliest English factories, the first manufacturing plants in America produced textiles. Soon, however, all kinds of goods were being made in U.S. factories. As the demand for these products increased, the factory owners looked for better and faster ways to manufacture them. Before long, they were using a system called mass production.

Eli Whitney is most often given credit for introducing the mass production techniques that changed the way goods were manufactured. In 1798 he assembled muskets using interchangeable parts in his factory in New Haven, Connecticut. For the first time, gun owners could buy replacement parts that would fit exactly with no need for custom fitting. Some gunsmiths found work cutting patterns for the parts, but others were put out of business because Whitney's mass-produced guns were much cheaper, lasted longer, and could be repaired more easily than handmade weapons.

Mass production took hold quickly. Soon it was used in the manufacture of clocks, furniture, and many other items. The use of interchangeable parts contributed to the growth of larger shops and factories, since a great many articles had to be produced in order for the interchangeable parts to be of value to the buyer. The mass production system also contributed to job specialization, and younger apprentices often repeated one or two small tasks over and over all day long, thereby learning much less about their craft.

Job Satisfaction Decreases
for Skilled Workers
As mass production techniques became more sophisticated, many skilled workers lost their livelihoods. Even if they were able to find employment in the new factories, they were forced to abandon their hard-earned skills and perform simple functions in front of machines. This led to discouragement and dissatisfaction.

Workers no longer owned their own tools as they did in earlier times. Now they operated machines that belonged to the factory owners. Often the workers never saw a completed product but spent all of their time repeating the few motions that the job required. A common complaint about factory work was that the repetition made it boring. As standardized parts and assembly lines came into being, workers became less interested in the product. Once that happened, the pride of workmanship was gone.

Factory Workers Suffer
As ownership of factories became concentrated in the hands of profit-minded investors, working conditions worsened. In the 1800s, the laws favored the business owners, and workers were not protected from financial disasters, industrial accidents, or unemployment. A growing number of factory workers lived at or below the poverty level. Until almost the beginning of the twentieth century, there was little attempt to regulate the conduct of the factory owners or to provide decent conditions for the workers.

Skilled workers were the ones who lost the most by the introduction of the factory system. Many factory owners refused to hire skilled craftsmen. Instead, they employed women, children, prisoners, and unskilled immigrants, who were less likely to protest poor working conditions and low wages. One-third to one-half of the labor force of New England between 1820 and 1830 consisted of children under the age of sixteen.

Cities grew around the factories. Some mill towns, such as Lowell, Massachusetts, owed their existence entirely to the new industries. The populations of cities such as Boston and New York doubled and then tripled very rapidly. The wealthy neighborhoods in these big cities had wide, paved, well-lighted streets, but the poorer sections were notorious for their poor sanitation, crime, and disease. The people who lived in these slums were blamed for the conditions of their neighborhoods, but they seldom owned the tenements in which they lived, and they felt powerless to change their lives as they struggled against hopelessness and poverty.

Workers were expected to operate their machines from dawn to sundown six days a week. They usually had four unpaid holidays a year, and no vacations. Factories often shut down for a week or two when the water was too low to power the machines or when there was not enough work, but employees were not paid during these shutdowns. It was extremely difficult for a family to save money since industrial accidents and illness resulted in complete loss of pay. Typically, the factory workers were at the mercy of the system that ensnarled them. They received little or no help from those who were better off, because the wealthier people of that time were often unsympathetic to or ignorant of the conditions that the lower classes endured. For example, in Fall River, Massachusetts, in 1855, a factory foreman told a visitor, "I regard my work people just as I regard my machinery. . . . When my machines get old and useless, I reject them and get new, and these people are part of my machinery."

Developing the West
As the Northeast became more highly industrialized, the frontier lands of the West attracted land-hungry pioneers who sought freedom and opportunity which older sections of the country did not offer. Many settlers found frontier life more attractive than working in factories of northern cities or on the farms in the South. For many, the West offered a better chance at social equality because on the frontier settlers were judged by their survival skills, not by their family backgrounds.

Trappers and traders pushed open the western parts of the continent. In colonial America, the fur trade was

*These children were employed in a typical
New England shoe factory in 1840.*

the largest industry, and it continued to be important throughout the nineteenth century. Fur traders were expert hunters who spoke Indian dialects, paddled canoes over rapids, set traps, skinned the dead animals, treated the pelts, and trekked back to civilization with their products. In the early nineteenth century, as cities were expanding in the East, trappers and traders in the western territories were breaking ground that would soon be filled with eager settlers.

The first pioneers cleared the frontier lands and built bridges and roads. Soon they built permanent homes and planted orchards. Small towns grew up with schools, mills, and sometimes libraries or theaters.

By 1840, pioneers had spread all over the Great Lakes area and into Michigan, Wisconsin, and Illinois. The industrial advances of the times brought inventions that made it possible to farm large, flat parcels of land. Farmers grew wheat and corn, raised hogs and shipped their crops and livestock east on the new railroads that linked the agricultural areas of the West with markets in the East. As the West prospered, the railroads brought carpenters and bricklayers. The towns attracted shopkeepers, bookkeepers, and traveling salesmen. While the basis of the economy was agriculture, there was enough extra wealth to support a civilized life. Soon there were larger stores, newspapers, lawyers, doctors, and politicians. By the middle of the nineteenth century, the frontier had moved on to the Southwest; the Midwest had become settled and civilized.

Transportation Workers

Transportation was vital to the settlement of the United States. Many men worked at occupations that involved building roads, digging canals, or laying railroads. The transportation lanes they constructed crisscrossed the whole continent, pulling the land closer together.

In the early 1800s, the United States entered into a period of roadbuilding and canal construction, especially along the Great Lakes and in the South. Some projects were privately financed; others were sponsored by the states or by the federal government. The single most important enterprise was the National Road, begun in 1811 and turned over to the states in 1853. By 1860, the section of the country east of the Mississippi River was crisscrossed by more than 3,000 miles of canals and 88,000 miles of surfaced roads.

Most of the canal and road workers were unskilled laborers. The Irish were the first immigrant laborers to fill the employment needs of an expanding country. Irish immigrants dug most of the Erie Canal, the most famous of the man-made waterways. Completed in 1825, it began at the Hudson River in Troy, New York, and stretched for 363 miles to Lake Erie at Buffalo, New York.

Farther west, on the Mississippi River, steamboats transported cargo from north to south. Steamers also plied the waters of the Great Lakes. Workers found jobs aboard the steamers and on the docks, loading and unloading cargo.

As transportation improved, the number of cartmen who carried goods in their wagons increased. Some cartmen simply hired themselves out to deliver goods, much as some truck drivers do today. Others became independent businessmen who bought and sold goods as they traveled from place to place. These peddlers stayed close on the heels of the pioneers as they pushed westward. Wherever Americans traveled, the peddlers were right behind them.

Steamboats and roads were vital to the development of the Northeast and the South, but it was the railroads that stimulated the development of the land west of the Mississippi. The first railroad was constructed in 1828, and by 1860 there were 30,000 miles of rails in the nation. Many of the railroads were laid by immigrant laborers who were willing to take the dangerous and backbreaking jobs others avoided.

Blasting rock often resulted in accidents and death, but at that time industrial accidents were simply considered hard luck for the worker. Employers provided no insurance, no sick pay, and no compensation for those who were maimed by explosives, nor did they aid families of men killed during Indian attacks.

Despite the hardships of working on the railroads, many men were grateful for the chance to earn a decent wage. In 1869, when the tracks were laid from east to west, over ten thousand men worked on the construction crews. The work gave these men their first view of the western lands, and when the railroads were finished, many of the workers bought cheap land in the regions to which their jobs had taken them.

A Nation Divided
The Industrial Revolution combined with western expansion to transform the American economy within a century. The differences between the northern and southern states grew more pronounced, and soon the Civil War tore the nation apart. When the war ended in 1865, the supremacy of the North was established, and industrial expansion continued rapidly. The period between 1865 and 1900 was characterized by traumatic change and labor struggles of violent proportions as well as great technical advances.

By 1900 the country had changed radically. The free lands of the West were almost completely settled, and the frontier was closed. Most manufacturing took place in large factories that employed mass production techniques. Some industries virtually disappeared because technology brought advances that made them unnecessary. The whaling industry, for example, died out when kerosene replaced whale oil as a lamp fuel, and blacksmithing became much less important as automobiles replaced the horse and wagon. At the same time, however, new industries grew up after the invention of photography and food processing and the discovery of rubber and electrical power.

The social and cultural changes that the Industrial Revolution brought were just as great as the technological and economic changes. Workers now depended on the machine for their subsistence instead of on their own tools and skills. They owned no land and had little hope of acquiring any. They lived in tenements and slums owned by shareholders as remote as those who owned the factories in which the laborers worked.

The artisan class of craftsmen who loved their work and signed or stamped each piece had virtually disappeared. Some social critics say that the Industrial Revolution turned workers into machines; others say the machine became the boss rather than the tool of the worker. The relationship between worker and product had changed, just as the relationship between employee and employer had undergone a radical readjustment. The workers' response to those changes was reflected in the rise of the labor movement.

3 | The Growth of Unions

In colonial days each worker made a bargain with his or her employer for wages and working conditions. The only organizations that existed were the guilds that master craftsmen formed to set prices and standards. The workers who organized these guilds were their own bosses, and their journeymen and apprentices had little say about working conditions or pay, so these organizations did not function as trade unions.

Although apprentices or journeymen didn't organize in colonial days, informal strikes called "turnouts" were common. These impromptu protests developed into worker organizations called societies, which journeymen began to form soon after the American Revolution. These societies attempted to aid employees as well as keep standards high. They also tried to set wage agreements and force employers to hire members of the society exclusively. By 1800, there were craftsmen's societies in carpentry, shoemaking, and printing.

These budding unions were declared illegal in 1806, however, when a Philadelphia judge ordered the shoemakers' association to disband. He said that one worker could bargain for higher wages, but if several employees banded together, it was a conspiracy. Nevertheless, skilled workers continued to organize and engage in turnouts, and labor organizations continued to grow. In 1842, the courts began to acknowledge that workers had the right to bargain collectively.

Industrial Revolution
Spurs Union Movement
The period from the 1820s to the 1850s saw many attempts to organize unions. But turnouts and strikes were

crushed quickly, and the workers' gains were slow in coming. Employees wanted to work no more than ten hours a day, and they commonly went on strike to show their bosses how strongly they felt about having to stay on the job from dawn to sundown. In 1836, the ten-hour-day movement achieved partial success when the national government agreed to allow workers at the Philadelphia Navy Yard to work only ten hours each day. Four years later the shorter workday was standard for all public employees.

The early labor movement suffered when economic depressions hit American businesses. Severe economic depressions caused unemployment, which made workers so afraid of losing their jobs that they could not risk engaging in strikes and turnouts. These periods of instability—sometimes called financial panics—had a devastating effect on factory workers, many of whom lost their jobs, took cuts in pay, or worked longer hours than usual. After the Panic of 1837, for example, the factory owners recovered after only three years of moderate hardship, but the workers never did regain their former security and prosperity.

Hard times disrupted union growth, and good times promoted it. Labor unions experienced some growth in the 1850s when the nation was in a period of prosperity, but most of their advances were wiped out during the Panic of 1857.

Trade unions went through another period of growth during the Civil War. Conflicts between workers and business became fiercer between 1861 and 1865 when more than a dozen new national unions were formed. By 1865, employees in many different occupations were organized on a national level. These unionized employees included cigarmakers, tailors, bricklayers, miners, and locomotive engineers.

Despite the growth of national unions, however, the

working classes made few gains in the 1860s. A *New York Times* survey of 1869 said that only one-eighth of the working class earned enough to afford "the comforts of life."

Established in 1866, the National Labor Union was the first really strong national union. It was made up of several different unions and reform movements. Its leader, William Sylvis, led the group to a peak membership of 600,000 in 1868. That same year, the National Labor Union was successful in pushing a law through Congress establishing an eight-hour workday for laborers and mechanics employed by the government.

The Panic of 1873, unsuccessful political activities of the union, and the death of William Sylvis weakened the National Labor Union, and it faded by 1875. However, it was the first workers' organization to exert real political influence. The annual sessions were especially noteworthy. They were the birthplace of the workers' general goals, which included the eight-hour day and abolition of child labor. Later workers' organizations would adopt these same goals.

Violence in the Labor Movement
The early labor movement was marked by violence on the part of both unions and management. One group that attained notoriety was the Molly Maguires, a secret union that was active in the Pennsylvania coal-mining region from 1852 to 1876. The members sabotaged plants. The leaders were eventually arrested, and ten were convicted of murder. Since all of the leaders of the Molly Maguires were Irishmen, the sensational newspaper accounts reinforced prejudices about immigrants and labor unions.

While few unions were as violent as the Molly Maguires, other bloody confrontations did occur, often with the federal government acting on behalf of business. In 1877, for example, President Hayes sent troops to reopen the railroad lines when Baltimore and Ohio Railroad workers struck. His action so infuriated American workers that work stoppages occurred all along the rail lines and in nearly every mill and mine in Pennsylvania, Ohio, and Indiana. This confrontation spread to Chicago, St. Louis, and San Francisco, and everywhere workers fought with federal troops and men hired by the railroad.

The union movement was synonymous with violence in the minds of many Americans who understood little of the desperation of the workers. Many Americans thought that all union organizers were murderers and criminals from foreign lands. Meanwhile, the workers continued to sweat in the filthy factories and starve as they waited for jobs, and they also continued to band together in their attempt to improve working conditions. Faced with formidable opposition from the federal government and unfair practices by their employers, workers sometimes resorted to desperate measures.

Though most newspaper coverage of the time emphasized the violent activities of the laborers, employers were also guilty of injustice. Management hired spies to infiltrate the unions and report the names of the leaders so they could be fired. Employers passed blacklists from one factory to another to ensure that a worker fired for union organizing in one place would not be hired to work in another.

Most owners and managers were indifferent to the fact that their workers did not earn enough to feed and clothe their families. The businessmen who controlled the new technology sometimes made huge fortunes while they exploited their employees. Cornelius Vanderbilt, for example, built a business empire from his steamships and railroads, and Andrew Carnegie was earning more than a million dollars a year from his steel and oil companies by the time he was thirty-four. These men and many others grew wealthy while their employees lived on low wages. Some of the most unscrupulous businessmen earned the name "Robber Barons."

These ruthless practices of management almost crippled the union movement and built deep enmity between ethnic groups, since the most recent immigrants were often used to break the strikes. Jay Gould, a millionaire investor who controlled the railroads in the Southwest, used this tactic to break a railroad strike in 1886. He said, "I can hire one-half of the working class to kill the other half."

Knights of Labor

The Knights of Labor, a union established in 1869, achieved wide popularity and touched the lives of many American workers. This organization attempted to organize skilled and unskilled workers as well as clerical and professional employees. The Knights of Labor had one million members by 1886 and exerted a tremendous influence on American politics. It effectively opposed child labor and Chinese immigration, but the issue that attracted the most attention was the demand for an eight-hour workday. Many parades and strikes gained workday concessions (usually nine hours) for 185,000 people.

Because the Knights of Labor was composed of workers from so many different occupations, however, there were disagreements among its members. By 1890, the membership of the Knights of Labor had dropped to 100,000. The group continued to fade until 1893, when the membership fell to 75,000.

AFL Begins

The American Federation of Labor (AFL) was formed in 1886 under the leadership of Samuel Gompers. At the age of ten, Gompers went to work as a cigarmaker, one of the lowest-paying occupations at the time. Like many other immigrants, he and his family lived in a crowded tenement in New York City, and the whole family worked at home rolling cigars.

Gompers entered union politics at the age of seventeen and became leader of the Cigarmakers' International Union in 1875. By 1881, he was active in a new national organization of workers called the Federation of Organized Trades, whose primary objective was to institute the eight-hour day.

In 1886 the Federation of Organized Trades was replaced by the American Federation of Labor, with Samuel Gompers and Peter McGuire as its leaders. Gompers continued as president of the AFL until his death in 1924. He is the best-known and most highly respected labor leader in American history.

Based on the belief that a separate union was needed for each type of work, the AFL was immediately attractive to the skilled workers who disliked being lumped with unskilled workers in the Knights of Labor.

The AFL built a tightly knit organization very quickly. It accepted only skilled craftsmen, and was remarkably well disciplined and organized. By 1900, the membership had climbed to 500,000 skilled workers.

Radical Groups Grow

Gompers and the AFL did a great deal for the skilled workers of America, but the union consistently excluded immigrants, blacks, and unskilled workers during its early years. While the Knights of Labor had been too inclusive, the early AFL was probably too exclu-

Samuel Gompers (center), is shown here with President Woodrow Wilson (left), and the U.S. Secretary of Labor at the dedication ceremony for the AFL building.

sive. Many unskilled workers looked to more radical organizations for help in improving their lives.

The Industrial Workers of the World (IWW) was formed in Chicago in 1905 in direct response to the AFL's exclusion of unskilled workers. The IWW's goals were as broad as those of the old Knights of Labor. Influenced by the radical political beliefs of Karl Marx, the union wanted to replace capitalism with a socialist system where the workers would own and control industry. Many people considered the IWW an "un-American" group because so many of its leaders were immigrants and because some of its members believed in radical political systems such as anarchism, communism, and socialism.

IWW strikes were often violent, and the press usually blamed the union for causing the trouble. One strike in Lawrence, Massachusetts, however, gained the sympathy of most of the nation. In Lawrence, 20,000 textile mill workers—mostly immigrants from Poland, Lithuania, Italy, and Russia—struck for higher wages. The strike lasted more than a month, and the strikers attempted to send their starving children to sympathetic communities. Although 211 children did go, after the third attempt, the local police refused to let the children leave. Desperate parents tried to put their sons and daughters on a train, but the police clubbed both mothers and children and dragged them away from the railroad station. The violence was reported in the newspapers and helped the workers win their strike.

While the IWW made some gains, the majority of American workers were attracted to the more conservative AFL. When the IWW refused to endorse the entry of the United States into World War I, it lost nearly all its influence. The leaders were prosecuted for treason, and one hundred members were sent to prison in 1918. From that time on, the IWW had no real strength.

Battle for Membership and Power

By the end of 1919, the AFL, with its policy of organizing according to crafts or occupations was the largest union group. However, there were always many independent groups that remained outside the AFL. The Railroad Brotherhood and the Federation of Amalgamated Clothing Workers were two such independent unions.

Competition between the independent unions and the AFL for membership was fierce, and much of the union organizers' energy went into trying to enlist individual workers.

Union membership doubled between 1915 and 1920 because of the curtailment of immigration during World War I and as a natural result of an economic boom that followed the war. Many disputes arose between unions over the right to organize workers, but there was also a move toward solidarity among workers as the anti-union forces began to gain ground once again.

The decade following World War I began with a series of strikes, many violent, that were opposed by government and business authorities. Court battles followed, and by 1922 the unions had lost the right to organize workers in many states. Effective political campaigns were waged against union rights, and many business leaders fought hard for the open shop, in which no union could force workers to join if they did not want to. Unions insisted that open shops were unfair and that all workers who benefited from collective bargaining should be required to support the organization that represented them. The anti-union open shop campaigns were very effective, and from 1920 until 1923, union membership declined from 5,047,800 to 3,622,000.

While unions lost some court fights, they won others. The Railway Labor Act of 1926 reinstated collective bargaining rights and prohibited discrimination against union members; it was a major gain.

Whatever gains unions made for workers in the 1920s were destroyed in the 1930s when the Great Depression brought unemployment to over 12 million people. The AFL and other unions were powerless to combat the extraordinary difficulties that resulted. Millions of workers lost their jobs and had to go on relief. Others accepted drastic wage cuts. By 1933 about one-fourth of the civilian labor force was out of work.

Great Depression
Brings Union Gains
The depression affected working people in every occupation. When President Franklin Delano Roosevelt took office in 1933, his first step was to devise a federal relief program to prevent people from starving.

In the spring of 1933, Roosevelt began two programs designed to revive business and increase employment: the National Recovery Administration and the Public Works Administration. He also created the Civilian Conservation Corps, a massive jobs program that put young men to work restoring the land. These programs and others were called the New Deal, and they heralded a new era for labor.

Because he was essentially pro-labor and because he needed the support of the labor movement, Roosevelt included in his new legislation the right to collective bargaining, and he denied companies the right to require members to join their own "company unions." These provisions were the basis for a powerful push toward organizing workers into unions.

The United Mine Workers, headed by John L. Lewis, organized all mine workers into one union, including machinists, pattern makers, boiler makers, carpenters, and miners. Unions of this kind were called "vertical unions" because they included all of the workers in a particular industry, both skilled and unskilled.

In 1935, John L. Lewis and other labor leaders formed a new organization called the Committee of Industrial Workers (CIO), after a dispute with the AFL. The name was later changed to the Congress of Industrial Workers. They then proceeded to organize several industries along vertical lines. The United Automobile Workers, for example, was a large union member of the CIO. The action taken by Lewis and the other CIO leaders resulted in their expulsion from the AFL. The CIO and the AFL remained separate organizations of almost equal power for over twenty years.

Other independent unions that made significant gains during the depression included the Amalgamated Clothing Workers and the Ladies' Garment Workers. During this time several new work areas were formed, including the American Newspaper Guild and the Screen Actors Guild.

Labor continued to gain strength during Roosevelt's administration. One significant step was the passage of the Wagner Act in 1935. Sponsored by Senator Robert F. Wagner of New York, the bill guaranteed the right to collective bargaining and provided for elections that would establish one union to represent workers in a plant. It set up a permanent National Labor Relations Board to administer the act and settle disputes between labor and management. It resulted in greater recognition of the rights of labor unions than ever before.

This legislation was buffered by the Fair Labor Standards Act, sometimes called the Wages and Hours Law, which was passed in 1938. It accomplished many goals that the labor unions had been working for during the past century. For example, it prohibited the employment of children under the age of sixteen in industries producing goods for interstate commerce, thereby essentially eliminating child labor. It also provided a maximum work week of forty-four hours in 1938, to be decreased to forty hours by 1940 with time-and-a-half pay for overtime work, and it set a minimum wage of 25 cents an hour in 1938, to be increased to 40 cents an hour in 1940. The law affected only workers in interstate industries, but there were about 13 million such workers in 1940, and the law's impact was nationwide.

World War II
When World War II began in Europe in 1939, American workers found that the long period of unemployment was over and there were jobs once again as American industry started manufacturing arms and supplies for Great Britain and Russia and building up its own national security. By the time the United States entered the war in December 1941, there was once again a shortage of skilled workers.

The full employment of the war years spurred union membership, and by the end of 1941, about one-fourth of the non–farm workers in the United States were union members.

Despite some disputes, labor, management, and government combined their energies to fight the Germans and Japanese. The wartime labor shortage opened new opportunities for women and blacks, and the government pushed through antidiscrimination measures. By the end of the war, over 14 million workers were union members, mostly in the AFL or CIO.

Postwar Unity
A wave of strikes hit the country as soon as the war was won. Workers had been restraining themselves

during the war effort, but they were now facing a normal workday. Many of them were accustomed to overtime paychecks, and they looked to the unions to help them avoid the cut in take-home pay.

Partly in response to the strikes and partly because the majority of Americans now viewed unions as too powerful, the Taft-Hartley Act was passed in 1947. An amendment to the Wagner Act, it outlawed the closed shop, jurisdictional strikes, and secondary boycotts. It also required union officials to sign noncommunist affidavits and allowed states to enact right-to-work laws.

Union members responded to this attack by moving toward greater solidarity within the worker ranks. After twenty years of disputing, the AFL merged with the CIO and formed the union that remains dominant in the United States today, the AFL–CIO. The merger was a gradual one, beginning in 1952. George Meany became president of the AFL in 1952 after the death of William Green. Meany led the two unions toward greater unity. Walter Reuther became president of the CIO in 1952, and they formed an even closer unit. In 1955, the merger became complete and George Meany became president of the AFL–CIO. The postwar age would bring new challenges to the union.

4

Black Workers

The Early Years

Black Americans hold a special place in the history of the American worker because such a large number of blacks were slaves until the Civil War.

Though slavery is the overwhelming fact in black American history, the first blacks who came to this continent were explorers, not slaves. There were blacks with Cortez when he conquered the Aztecs, and with Ponce de León when he discovered Florida. Estaban Dorantes, a black explorer, was among the first to explore California in 1528 and was directly responsible for the exploration of Arizona and New Mexico. He was a leader like many other blacks who came to the Americas with the Spanish and Portuguese colonists.

The blacks who settled in the Southwest intermarried. Most of their descendants became a part of the general population without preserving a separate identity. In certain parts of Mexico, especially along the coast, a large number of people have curly hair and other African characteristics, but little remains beyond that.

Slavery Is Established

In 1619, the first blacks who came to Virginia were bound servants with the same rights as the white bound servants. They worked for a period of time and then were free. Only twenty blacks were in that first group of bound laborers, but there were half a million black slaves in America by the time of the Revolution.

Slavery became common in the 1640s. During the 1660s and 1670s, the southern states enacted a series of harsh laws known as the Black Codes. This collection of laws recognized slavery as legal and restricted the mobility of slaves. This code also decreed that the children of slaves would inherit the condition of slavery. In other words, a child born to a black slave woman was the property of the mother's owner.

Slaves were acquired as a part of a triangular trade pattern between New England, Africa, and the West Indies or the southern colonies, usually by English or New England sea captains who traded guns, food, textiles, rum, and utensils to West African chiefs who delivered the slaves they had taken captive from other tribes.

Traveling across the ocean in those days was difficult for all immigrants, but the conditions that the African blacks endured were horrendous. They were packed, two by two, in chains in such crowded conditions that they seldom could lie down full-length. Shipboard epidemics sometimes killed everyone, and it was normal for a fourth or more to die during the crossing. Often, the Africans tried to commit suicide by jumping overboard, and some mothers threw their babies into the sea so that they could escape slavery.

Most whites did not know about the terrible travel conditions, but there was always controversy over the morality of slavery. The Quakers, who settled Pennsylvania, always opposed slavery, and many other Americans considered the slave trade a disreputable way to earn a living.

Plantation owners who bought slaves to work on their large establishments justified slavery as necessary for their agricultural economy. The large plantations of the South, which grew tobacco, rice, and indigo, gradually came to depend entirely on black slave labor. By the time of the American Revolution slavery was well established and restricted to those with African ancestry. Over 85 percent of the blacks lived in the South, and more than three-fifths of them were concentrated in Virginia and the Carolinas.

Although there had been attempts to abolish slavery since the late seventeenth century, the U.S. Constitution recognized the existence of slavery and did not forbid the importation of slaves until the year 1808.

Despite the constitutional protection of slavery, it remained a regional institution. Perhaps if slaves could have been used more profitably in the North, slavery would also have been established there, but the smaller northern farms made that impractical. Slavery was abolished in the northern states very early, and the Northwest Ordinance of 1787 forbade slavery in the western frontier territory.

The laws governing slavery were designed to limit the freedom of blacks, not to protect their rights. Though these laws varied, they all prohibited slaves from leaving their owners' premises without written permission. Slaves could not legally make contracts, and their testimony was inadmissible in any court case involving a white person. They could not own property, be taught how to read or write, or assemble unless a white person was present. While these laws were not always enforced, the slaves were at the mercy of their owners.

Slaves worked not to improve their own position in life but to improve the fortune of their owners. If they attempted to rebel, they were severely punished. Some were sold away from their families or even killed.

Although white factory workers in the North also endured many hardships and deprivations, they had some chance to improve their conditions. Most slaves had almost no hope of improving their lives no matter how hard they worked. On some plantations, physical conditions in which slaves lived and worked were no worse than those in industrial cities, but slavery was destructive and demoralizing, nevertheless, because people were treated as property.

Even in the North where slavery was illegal, the property rights of southern slave owners were respected, and the law required the return of runaway slaves. So, in order to be safe, a slave had to make his or her way far north into Canada.

Despite the rigidity of the laws and the fact that most blacks were kept at the lowest level of poverty and ignorance, some slaves attained a high degree of skill and education. One visitor to the South in 1840 found that slaves were "trained to every kind of manual labor. The blacksmith, cabinetmaker, carpenter, builder, wheelwright all have one or more slaves laboring at their trades."

As the Industrial Revolution brought new machines, blacks worked at every industrial occupation; they became mechanics, machinists, shoemakers, bakers, printers, papermakers, textile workers, salt boilers, and steamboat men. They built bridges and dug coal; they chopped wood and hauled cargoes.

By 1860, approximately 500,000 slaves lived in cities and worked in urban occupations, but the vast majority of the nation's 4 million slaves worked as field hands on plantations. They labored long hours cultivating and harvesting cotton, rice, tobacco, and other crops. The slaves had to stoop or bend for hours at a time, often in the extreme heat of the midday sun. Plantation owners and managers were constantly searching for ways to bring down the cost of producing cotton and other crops, and it was usually the slaves who suffered from their economy measures. When the demand for cotton was high, the slaves' only return for their increased labor was harsher working conditions, longer hours, and tougher overseers who pushed the workers to the limit by using cruel punishments and physical violence. Whipping a worker to death was rare because slaves were expensive, but beatings and whippings were legal and common forms of punishment.

Living conditions in slave quarters were usually very poor though they varied according to the size of the farm and the temperament of the owner. As a rule, only the barest essentials for the subsistence of the slaves were provided. Food was simple, and clothing was made of the cheapest materials or consisted of hand-me-downs. Many blacks were housed in crude huts that barely protected them from the weather.

While the majority of the slaves accepted their lot with no outward manifestation of dissatisfaction, some planned and executed revolts. Others resisted by destroying farm implements or animals. Some ran away by themselves or with the help of friendly whites in the North or brave blacks, but the long journey north to Canada was an impossibility for most. Those black slaves who gained freedom by legal means had only two choices: to stay in the South or to abandon everyone they loved. Running away, of course, meant never seeing their families again. About half of the approximately 500,000 free blacks lived in the slave states in 1860 despite the fact that the laws that governed them were almost as severe as the slave codes.

Opposition to slavery had begun almost as soon as the first Africans were brought to the country. By 1790, many people believed that slavery should be abolished altogether. These abolitionists, as they were called, objected to slavery on moral grounds. Two early Presidents, George Washington and Thomas Jefferson, though slaveholders themselves, went on record as being against slavery. Jefferson freed most of his slaves at his death, and Washington's slaves were freed at his wife's death.

For a while in the late 1700s, it looked as though slavery might die a natural death. The great plantations were producing fewer crops, and it looked as though slavery might not be profitable much longer. The land was wearing out, and the cost of feeding and clothing slaves was the same or greater.

Then the invention of the cotton gin by Eli Whitney in 1793 fastened slavery's grip on the black worker for another seventy years. Whitney's machine quickly separated the seeds from the cotton fibers, which meant that cotton could be produced in greater amounts more cheaply. The new methods of processing along with the expansion of textile mills produced a greater demand for raw cotton. In 1791 the total American production of cotton fiber was only 400 bales. By 1830 it was up to 732,000 bales, and by 1860 production had reached 5,387,000 bales, two-thirds of the total cotton production of the world, all of it produced by slave labor.

As a consequence of the increased demand for cotton, slaves were also in demand. Despite the prohibition against importing new slaves, blacks were smuggled in from the Caribbean and Africa illegally. Slaves were also encouraged to increase their own population. At the height of the cotton boom, the cost of a prime field hand—a healthy male between fifteen and twenty-five years of age—rose to $1,800 on the New Orleans slave market.

In spite of the Industrial Revolution, most blacks continued to work in the fields in exactly the same way that earlier slaves had, using hand tools, wearing hand-woven clothing, and eating home-grown food.

Eli Whitney's cotton gin made cotton a profitable commodity in the southern United States and raised the demand for slave labor to tend the crop.

Free Blacks of the North
By 1860 there were about 500,000 free blacks living in
America, with more than half living in northern cities
such as New York and Boston. Though technically free,
they encountered great prejudice and hostility, and most
were restricted to menial jobs as laborers or servants.
Nevertheless, from the earliest colonial period, blacks
had some educational and training opportunities, and
they were allowed to organize some social and religious institutions of their own.

A few fortunate or enterprising blacks were able to
establish small businesses and prosper. Some blacks
worked in every trade and occupation, but most were
hampered by lack of education, training, and capital.
Their lack of formal education essentially kept blacks out
of the professions altogether. Institutions of higher
learning in the North were for whites only. The first
schools for blacks were usually established by Quakers.

As the abolitionist movement grew, the opposition
to it also hardened. Much of the conflict stemmed from
workers' fears that the freed blacks would compete for
white laborers' jobs. During the 1840s it was common
for abolitionist meetings to be broken up by northern
workers who feared competition from black labor.

Job competition was fierce, and workers in the North
already feared being replaced by machines or by immigrants. They were determined not to have to also
compete with blacks. Opposition to the abolition of
slavery grew strong in the North. One abolitionist
leader, William Lloyd Garrison, said that he "found
contempt more bitter, opposition more stubborn, and
apathy more frozen" in New England than in the South.
Despite opposition, however, the abolitionist movement grew and the number of black workers in the
North increased.

Frontier Settlers

While the conflict between the North and the South intensified and moved toward war, the West was being settled by enterprising men and women, some of whom were blacks. Blacks had been on the frontier since the beginning, when the fur trade was the main industry of colonial America. Some black slaves came west with their owners and eventually escaped; others were free people who sought the open spaces of the frontier.

Black fur traders had a special aptitude for dealing with Indians, and many blacks married Indians or became members of a tribe. Today, many American blacks can trace their heritage all the way back to the Indians and former slaves of colonial times.

Because of their special affinity for dealing with Indians, blacks were often invaluable as interpreters. Other blacks found work as cowboys in the West. Their sympathy with the Indians and the democratic attitudes of the white frontiersmen made the West a logical place for enterprising young men who had the necessary stamina and courage to survive on the edge of the wilderness.

One famous black cowboy was Britton Johnson, who was considered the best shot on the Texas frontier immediately after the Civil War. Unlike some other blacks, his allegiance was to the white settlers, not the Indians in the area. Comanche and Kiowa Indians attacked his home, killing his youngest son and kidnapping his wife and three surviving children. Johnson posed as a warrior recruit and pretended to join the outlaw band of Indians. By doing this, he managed to free his family and several white captives.

In addition to the fur traders, explorers, and cowboys, there were black pioneer settlers. One group of 385 freed blacks settled in Mercer County, Ohio in 1832; they were probably the first large group of black pi-

Some free blacks such as these in a drawing by
Frederic Remington, found work on the western
frontier as scouts, interpreters, and cowboys.

oneers. Later, in 1901, their descendants formed the Randolph Slave Society to honor their ancestors.

As the American Indians were pushed off their lands and forced farther west, blacks often joined them so as to escape from slavery. Large numbers of black men and women fled to Indiana by hiding among bands of Indians as they were forced to leave North Carolina. In 1831, an army census showed that 512 blacks lived with the Choctaw tribe. That count may be inaccurate, however, since it was based on the census-takers' impressions of physical appearance.

Some runaway slaves were recaptured and returned to their owners. As a rule, that task was left to professional slave hunters who received a bounty for each slave. Because it was difficult for the slave hunters to match descriptions, most escaped blacks were allowed to remain with the Indians. In fact, one tribe included so many blacks that white settlers asked the government to take away their land.

The alliance of Indians and blacks is easy to understand because the prejudice against both groups was intense. Black settlers were able to find free farmland in some parts of the West, but they endured a great deal of prejudice, especially when they began to settle in larger groups.

Discriminatory laws against blacks moved into the West with the white settlers. In 1803, Indiana passed a law prohibiting blacks from giving testimony against whites in courts of law. The other territories followed with a variety of laws against blacks, though they were not always enforced. When public schools came to the West, they were usually segregated, and there was little or no social or business commerce between whites and blacks. Despite the barriers set against them, however, many blacks established homes in the West and lived traditional lives of pioneers.

By 1890 there were half a million blacks in Texas and Oklahoma, and many more lived in Kansas and Nebraska. Trappers, Indian recruits, pioneers, or cowboys, these blacks carved a place for themselves in the West despite opposition.

After the Civil War
Farmers Lose the Battle
The abolition of slavery was only one cause of the Civil War, which began in 1861. Economic rivalry and resentment tore the North and South apart. At the same time, the debate about whether or not slaves should be freed raged until President Abraham Lincoln signed the Emancipation Proclamation on January 1, 1863, declaring that all slaves that were in rebellion against the Union would be free. When the war ended in 1865, 4 million blacks were free for the first time in their lives. Most of them had been born in slavery and were not prepared to survive on their own. They looked to the government for help.

The southern economy was in chaos at the end of the war, and many of the newly freed workers were unprepared to earn a living. Most were unskilled field hands who had never learned a craft and could not read and write. The government established the Freedmen's Bureau to help reconstruct the South, and free food and clothing were distributed to both whites and blacks. Attempts to start schools for blacks and institute training programs, however, encountered tremendous problems. Rumors that every former slave would get "forty acres and a mule" for Christmas kept a lot of blacks from asking their former masters for work. The plantation owners had land but little seed and no money to pay their former slaves. Thousands of blacks wandered throughout the South, begging for odd jobs.

Out of fear and in response to the economic chaos, southerners insisted on a new set of laws to restrict the newfound liberty of blacks. The resultant laws varied, but basically, they protected the pattern of discrimination, which had begun in slavery and would continue throughout the South for a century.

Some blacks managed to acquire farmland, but for the most part, working conditions were hardly changed from the time of slavery. Free, but with little education and no help from the whites, thousands of blacks had no choice but to work on plantations. The old slave quarters now housed black workers who were paid very little. For some, freedom actually brought worse conditions, because they now had to buy their own food and clothing and repair their own homes.

Most blacks continued to work as field hands on large plantations or as tenant farmers. Three-fourths of the blacks living on farms were tenants who paid rent or sharecroppers who received a share of the profit from the crops they grew. This system often created a vicious cycle, for most sharecroppers were so poor they were compelled to ask for credit from the white merchants in order to survive. This meant that they bought food, clothing, tools, and farm implements at prices 40 to 100 percent higher than those charged by noncredit stores. Once this cycle of credit buying was established, most poor farmers lived and died in debt.

By 1900, nearly 193,000 blacks owned farms, but these farmers had trouble avoiding credit buying. They remained in debt because of crop failures, droughts, and lack of education and management skills. In some parts of the South, 90 percent of the black farmers were in debt to white merchants. Many were forced to mortgage their farms, and those who failed to pay off their mortgages would lose their land. Gradually, many thousands of black farmers lost their land to wealthier white merchants. Often, the blacks stayed on as tenant farmers or sharecroppers, getting deeper and deeper into debt and despair.

Nonagricultural Work Declines
After the Civil War the number of occupations open to blacks actually declined as white southerners hardened the lines of discrimination and refused to hire blacks as blacksmiths or mechanics even if they had performed that same work skillfully when they were slaves. The overwhelming majority of blacks were confined to agricultural work. At the same time, though, a class of black professionals quickly grew out of the new schools that the Quakers and other reformers opened. This professional class was very small, but it provided black leaders who eventually set the stage for change.

Blacks had a great deal of trouble establishing a place in the union movement. For many years they were systematically excluded from membership. The resistance to blacks was increased when employers used them to break the strikes of union members. Finally, in 1869, blacks were seated at the convention of the National Labor Union after a furious debate. That same year blacks formed a union of their own and elected Isaac Myers president. Called the National Colored Labor Union, the organization lasted for six years and was active in the struggle for the eight-hour day for all workers. This group also worked to obtain rights for women as well as for blacks.

In the late nineteenth century, the Knights of Labor admitted blacks to its ranks. The Industrial Workers of the World adopted this policy in the early twentieth century. Both organizations eventually included many black workers, but no black leaders. Later on, the AFL excluded black skilled workers or segregated them into separate unions. This discrimination continued in the AFL well into the 1950s.

Because industry, small shops, and the skilled trades were closed to them, many blacks who did not want to be servants or field hands looked to the railroads for employment. From the mid-1800s, the railway companies had hired blacks to work as porters, or redcaps, carrying and loading packages and luggage. Blacks were not given skilled jobs on the railroads, however, and when the American Railway Union was formed in 1893, it excluded blacks altogether. As a result, black railroad workers eventually formed their own union under the leadership of A. Philip Randolph.

World War I Brings
Opportunities and Change
The first opportunity for blacks to enter northern industry in large numbers came during World War I. The war brought increased production needs, and a severe labor shortage occurred when thousands of young men left their jobs to fight in the army. Immigration was halted during the war, and that added to the shortage of workers. This labor crisis meant that new jobs were available to blacks in iron and steel mills, coal mines, and automobile factories. Many southern blacks moved northward, abandoning the impoverished southern farms.

Depression and the New Deal
The Great Depression of the 1930s brought hardship to all workers, but blacks suffered more than any other ethnic group because they were the ones who had made the most recent entry into the labor force. The policy of letting people go according to how long they had

worked for the company was widespread, and the use of this seniority system meant that blacks were consistently fired before whites. The slogan "Last hired, first fired" eliminated any hope that blacks had for continued employment as 10 million workers—black and white—lost their jobs.

While northern blacks were losing their industrial employment, the blacks on farms were suffering equally frightening setbacks. A series of bad farming years in the twenties and thirties combined with the depression economy to hasten the failure of independent ownership of farms and to force more and more blacks into the position of tenants or sharecroppers.

Though New Deal legislation instituted by President Roosevelt was not specifically directed toward blacks, it gave them a great deal of relief. The New Deal farm measures were considered radical at that time because they took millions of acres out of production and created an artificial scarcity of products to drive prices up. The farmer who did not plant crops was paid "benefit payments," or subsidies, for letting the land lie fallow.

These agricultural policies earned Roosevelt a tremendous amount of criticism. But the policies were effective in bringing the farmer a better standard of living. Roosevelt also instituted the Soil Conservation and Domestic Allotment Act, which gave benefit payments to farmers who cooperated with a soil conservation program, and the Bankhead–Jones Act of 1937, which was a direct help to tenant farmers, sharecroppers, and migratory workers. This act authorized the Farm Security Administration to make loans at very low interest rates to farmers who wanted to buy land. By 1940, some 13,000 farmers had bought land through the Bankhead–Jones program.

The most important piece of New Deal legislation for farmers, black as well as white, was the Agricultural Adjustment Act of 1938. It provided benefits for farmers who withdrew lands from production. It also allowed the government to restrict the amounts of crops participating farmers could produce and to store surplus production, and it provided price supports, loans, and other financial assistance to participating farmers.

Black workers benefited greatly from New Deal farm measures because most blacks were still agricultural workers. And they also benefited from the many legislative acts designed to improve the position of industrial workers. Legislation such as the Fair Labor Standards Act, the Work Progress Administration, and the other New Deal legislation helped black Americans.

World War II Brings
More Big Changes
World War II not only brought an end to the Great Depression; it also revolutionized the position of black workers in the United States. During the war, many blacks moved from southern farms to northern and southern factories. The migration of blacks was spurred by the war and the development of technical advances in agriculture.

After 1939, blacks entered the industrial labor force in great numbers, and the migration from rural to urban areas began to speed up. There was far from full equality in the workplace, but blacks now worked in occupations that had been closed to them before. They found jobs in every type of factory including steel making, shipbuilding, and airplane manufacture. Often their jobs were the lowest paid, and their working conditions were the worst, but for the first time, they were admitted to skilled industrial occupations, not relegated to menial labor. They were also able to break discriminatory barriers in several nonindustrial occupations, and many of them became beauticians, barbers, cooks, counter clerks, and waiters.

Under the leadership of President Roosevelt, black workers made significant gains by the time the war ended in 1945. During the Roosevelt years, executive orders declared that there would be no discrimination in industries working on government contracts, and federal jobs began to open up for black workers, many of whom found work in the Postal Service.

The end of the war did not mean a loss of all gains, as it had after World War I. The Presidents who followed Roosevelt continued to press for fair employment practices and to eliminate patterns of discrimination in work. President Truman, who assumed the presidency after Roosevelt died in 1945, fought hard for civil rights legislation and risked an open breach with southern white leaders of the Democratic party.

The 1950s brought a significant gain for workers when the Supreme Court declared that segregated education was not equal and that schools in the South must be combined to serve both black and white students. Until that time educational opportunities for blacks had been very limited because most attended segregated schools where the amount of money spent on black students was as little as a third of that spent on whites.

The desegregation of schools was controversial, and many confrontations arose over this and other civil rights issues. While progress appeared very slow to blacks and to white liberals, tremendous changes did take place for black people during the decades following World War II, particularly in the area of work.

A series of laws and proclamations against discrimination was capped by the Fair Employment Practices Act of 1964 (Title VII of the Civil Rights Act of 1964). This act made it illegal for any employer to discriminate against anyone on the basis of race, and blacks immediately began to apply for positions that had been closed to them before. Managers' and foremen's jobs, insurance sales and publishing jobs, industrial engineering and countless other occupations opened up.

Blacks began to take legal action against employers who discriminated, and they made gains through court decisions in class action suits in which several blacks would sue on behalf of a larger group. The federal government now insists that employers who benefit from government contracts must employ a fair percentage of minority workers. This has spurred companies to search for qualified black managers as well as laborers.

Unions Open Up
Many unions excluded blacks until the fifties when government and public pressure forced them to open their membership to blacks. The admission of blacks in larger numbers came as a part of the changes that attended the merger of the AFL and CIO. Under the leadership of George Meany, the number of black members in the AFL–CIO reached 2 million by 1955.

The acceptance of blacks into labor unions, however, came at a time when the need for skilled and unskilled workers was declining in the United States. As before, recently hired black union members often were the first to be laid off as unemployment hit one industrial segment after another. Though the policies of the unions were growing more liberal, the number of jobs was decreasing, and so the blacks continued to suffer from that old rule, "Last hired, first fired."

Many job opportunities open to young blacks in the

early 1980s were for skilled positions that required higher training. Because of educational deficiencies, young blacks faced unemployment even during times when there were job openings. Without the training, they did not qualify for positions as computer operators, hospital technicians, or other skilled workers.

Unemployment among young blacks who had not completed high school was often as high as 40 percent, and no easy solutions to the problem had been found. Several job training programs were specifically designed by the federal government to help disadvantaged youth, and some of the programs seemed to help young people.

Faced with an increasingly complex job market and a growing need for technical skills, young blacks who would have become unskilled workers twenty years ago now find that those positions no longer exist. Their education in substandard schools, plus a long history of discrimination and despair, have not equipped them to compete with other workers. Black workers have made many gains, but they have a long way to go before they truly enjoy equal opportunity with whites.

5 | *Immigrants Seek Opportunity*

Moving from one country to another in search of a better life is as old as the human race. Even the American Indians are descendants of immigrants; it is believed that their ancestors gradually worked their way from Asia, moving across a land bridge that once connected the Soviet Union and Alaska.

The first European settlers on the Atlantic Coast of North America were from England, and they made their settlements in the New World as much like English villages as possible. Those settlers brought English law, English dress, and English customs to the new land.

Immigrants from Holland colonized New Netherlands in 1624, and at the height of its influence, about 10,000 Dutch settlers lived under the control of the Dutch West India Company. By 1665, the Dutch had extended their influence by taking over New Sweden, a smaller colony along the Delaware River.

The English gained control of New Netherlands in 1664 and renamed it New York. Although the Dutch and Swedish influence remained, the colonies became primarily English. During the eighteenth century, the English came to the American colonies in larger and larger numbers; about 1½ million of them settled on the East Coast from Maine to Georgia.

Settlers came from other lands, too. Many Scottish immigrants settled here, mostly in the South. They blended so well with the English that the two groups were almost indistinguishable from each other. Most of the French-speaking immigrants came to America through Canada, rather than directly from Europe, and they came in great numbers. Significant numbers of

Germans and Irish made the difficult crossing to America to find a better life than they had in Europe, where conditions were steadily deteriorating.

Some immigrants, as we know, came as indentured servants and filled unskilled labor slots. But many others, especially those who came from countries other than England, were skilled artisans who continued to ply their trades in the new land. These non-English immigrants tended to settle in specific areas and specialize in certain kinds of work. The Italians worked in Georgia on silk culture; the Polish worked in Virginia in the shipyards; the Dutch set up sawmills in New York State; and the French cultivated vineyards in the Northeast. Irish textile workers defied English bans and set up a linen industry in New England and Maryland.

The immigration flow was small and steady during the seventeenth and eighteenth centuries, bringing people from most European nations, but basically from England. After the American Revolution, the flow diminished dramatically. In the first years between 1790 and 1830, the population tripled, reaching a total of 13 million people, but that increase resulted chiefly from the high birth rate. Only 400,000 people immigrated here from Europe during those early years.

Immigration Increases

After 1830, immigration increased steadily until it was curtailed in the 1920s. The first immigrants had been mostly skilled craftsmen, but many later immigrants were less skilled workers who were fleeing worse conditions at home.

Nearly every immigrant wanted to work, and this caused tension between native-born workers and newcomers. Part of the conflict resulted from a lack of understanding of the causes of unemployment. Many native-born workers did not understand that they were being displaced because of the tremendous changes in manufacturing that caused the mechanization of their jobs. They resented the immigrants, who were willing to work for less money. Established workers grew angry because their demands for higher wages and better working conditions were threatened by immigrants who were eager to accept any work at all. The competition between native-born workers and immigrants became intense as immigration increased and resentment boiled over when immigration reached its height between 1880 and 1910. At that time, the worker population expanded one-third faster than the total population. The working population showed a net increase of 25 million between 1870 and 1910, and 20 percent of it was due to immigration.

The waves of immigrants continued as hardships at home drove them to the United States. Europe underwent a century of turbulent political and industrial change, stemming from the same causes that had affected American workers. In Europe, however, these changes affected the lives of the workers much more severely because of entrenched political oppression and the absence of economic opportunity.

Germans came here in larger numbers after 1815, mostly because of a series of political conflicts. Others came strictly for economic reasons, often because of glowing letters from the friends and relatives who had preceded them.

Primarily farmers, the Germans first settled in Maryland, Pennsylvania, and upper New York State. Later, they moved into Ohio, Michigan, Illinois, and Missouri. Buffalo, Cleveland, Chicago, and Kansas City still have large German communities.

Since colonial days, Germans have been active in

every craft and trade in America. The later immigrants found factory work, especially as brewers and meat packers in the Midwest. German beer and sausage makers are still a colorful part of our ethnic makeup. Most Germans, however, settled on their own land, eventually intermarried with their English and Scottish neighbors, and became part of the general Northern European mixture that we sometimes still refer to as "All-American." The Germans escaped some of the resentment and hostility that greeted other immigrants. There were several reasons for this: (1) many Germans had a little wealth when they came; (2) most of them were Protestants; (3) they earned a reputation for hard work; and (4) they spread out over the landscape.

The Irish started arriving in large numbers at about the same time as the Germans, but the famines and economic troubles in their homeland forced even greater numbers of them to come to America. Often, they were starving when they arrived. Without the resources to become landowners, they congregated in northern cities, inhabiting the first American slums. Between 1830 and 1840, over half a million immigrants came to America and almost half of them were Irish.

Often they stayed in or near the cities where they landed, Boston or New York, because they did not have the money to move on. Many lived in hovels, in basements, or on the streets. These Irish immigrants had no skills, and few factory owners would hire them. In Lowell, Massachusetts, for instance, the Yankee farm girls who worked in the mills consistently refused to work with Irish. The Irish who lived there found work digging canals, building streets, or working as servants, but they were not allowed inside the factories. They were segregated into one small area of Lowell called "The Acre." There were no sewers in that section, and garbage and filth ran in open ditches down the streets.

The barriers of prejudice against the Irish were strong, partly because of their Catholic religion. Nearly all of the early settlers had been Protestant, and though the Constitution guaranteed freedom of religion, many Protestants were suspicious of Catholics. They believed the Catholics had to do what the Pope in Rome told them to do and could not be loyal citizens.

Despite the hardships here, the Irish continued to migrate in large numbers because the conditions at home were so much worse. Ireland was basically an agricultural nation ruled by English landlords. Most of the poor tenants lived almost exclusively on potatoes because they were the one crop that would grow on the poor soil allowed to the tenants.

The failure of the potato crop in 1846 caused a massive evacuation of that land. The blight continued to rot the potatoes for several years, causing widespread starvation among the peasants. Under British rule, the Irish tenant farmers were helpless, and nearly everyone who could get together passage money made the trip to America. In earlier years, Irish immigration had been growing slowly. The number who immigrated in 1843 was 20,000, but the potato famine increased the urgency of immigration. In 1851 the number was up to 220,000 for just that one year.

Many Irish workers found employment in the transportation industry—digging canals, laying roads, and building railroads. Thousands of them became servants in the homes of well-to-do Americans. Later, employers were willing to give them factory jobs if they would accept low enough wages. Even the Lowell textile factories eventually began to employ Irish workers in large numbers after a series of strikes by the Yankee girls that began in 1836. The strikers were defeated, and the Irish almost completely took over the textile mills of New England.

The Irish lived in the northeastern cities, especially Boston and New York. Many immigrants worked in factories, but their sons sought work that offered more money and power. Many entered politics or sought government jobs. So many Irishmen became policemen by the turn of the century that the Irish cop had become a stereotype frequently seen in plays and, later, movies. Eventually descedants of the Irish entered every trade and business and achieved a place in the American mainstream. When an Irish-American, John F. Kennedy, became President of the United States, it was clear that all of the old barriers had crumbled.

The Challenges of Assimilation
As immigration increased, so did resistance to the immigrants. Native-born Americans complained that the immigrants did not try to fit themselves into the culture quickly enough. At the same time, however, they tried to deprive the immigrants of jobs, educational opportunities, and civil rights. Eventually, the Germans and the Irish did become a part of the culture by adopting English-American customs; that process is called assimilation.

Assimilation is a concern of every immigrant group. As the newcomers struggle to achieve the same standard of living that other Americans enjoy, they must learn new ways of living and thinking, and often a new language as well. The problems of immigrants in a new society are always great, but the ease with which they assimilate depends partly on how close their culture is to the American one. English and Scottish immigrants had the easiest time because they spoke the same lan-

This early print shows the construction of the Erie Canal
in New York State, work that was performed
largely by Irish immigrants.

guage and followed the customs of most native-born Americans. The Irish spoke the same language, but their uneducated speech, their poverty, their peasant-like behavior, and their Catholic religion created a barrier. Northern Europeans such as Germans and Scandinavians suffered less discrimination than later immigrants from southern and eastern Europe.

The Industrial Revolution affected industrial workers in northern Europe and America, causing unemployment and immigration. It also forced unskilled workers from southern and eastern Europe to immigrate in the second half of the nineteenth century. In these parts of Europe there was little industry and few new farming machines. The technological advances in agriculture in America affected European workers, who could not compete with farmers in the United States. In 1887 the wheat farms of the northwestern United States could produce wheat for 40¢ a bushel, and farm workers earned $25.00 a month. In eastern Europe, wages were $6.00 a month, but the cost of production was 80¢ a bushel. Despite the fact that workers earned much less, they lost employment because the European wheat farms could no longer compete with American ones. Since there was no work in their homelands, many workers sold everything they had to buy passage to America where they hoped to obtain any kind of work at all.

The Industrial Revolution in Europe created problems that were compounded by political turmoil. The troubles in Ireland and Germany continued to propel immigration from those lands, and those immigrants were joined by thousands of others from the South and East.

Large numbers of people began to arrive from Scandinavia, Czechoslovakia, Austria, Hungary, and later Greece and Italy. After 1880 more immigrants came from the eastern and southern parts of Europe than from the North, and these newcomers encountered a great deal more resistance than the Germans and Irish had. The new arrivals were for the most part poor and uneducated, and their languages and cultures were very different from those of America. They also had more trouble assimilating because they came in such large numbers, and hostility toward them hardened as workers fought for jobs. Talk of restricting immigration gained momentum, especially as the stronger labor unions such as the AFL gained ground.

Organized Resistance
to Immigration
Organized resistance to immigration arose almost as soon as the number of immigrants noticeably increased. There were local riots and conflicts, often between labor union members and immigrants. As immigration kept increasing, the resistance hardened into a national political organization called the Native American party, better known as the Know-Nothing party.

The Native American party was organized in 1845; its members supported only native-born Protestant Americans for political office and opposed all foreigners. The American party was able to elect nearly all of the public officials in Massachusetts in 1854, but the organization eventually lost its strength because it split over the slavery question and because increased immigration changed the political makeup of the nation.

The group of workers who had the most difficult time assimilating were the Chinese who were imported to this country to work on the first transcontinental railroad, which was completed in 1869. The first group of 13,000 Chinese came in 1854 to mostly work the gold mines, and by the mid-1870s there were over 100,000 here. Chinese laborers who worked in railroad construction crews performed the most dangerous, difficult work possible, and many died in the blasting operations used to cut a path through the Rocky Mountains. Others died from malnutrition, disease, and overwork. Despite the nearly inhuman working conditions, Chinese men came here eagerly because they were so poor at home.

For these early construction crews, assimilation was not an issue, since many of the Chinese workers hoped to return to China eventually. The Chinese stayed together in the beginning, and their leaders exerted great efforts to keep their religious and cultural lives free of Western influence. Some Chinese workers did return home, but others elected to remain here. They found work as miners, cooks, and small businessmen when the railroad was completed. Some brought their brides to this country, and most settled in California, especially in the San Francisco area, where their influence is still very strong. Others moved on to Hawaii to work on the sugar plantations and eventually married other immigrants or Hawaiian natives.

The Chinese represented 20 percent of the California labor force in 1870, and the other workers bitterly resented them because they worked for the lowest wages. The Chinese were considered very different and were always segregated from other workers. As a result, it was easy for hatred and suspicion to build. When the Financial Panic of 1873 hit the nation, anger against the Chinese acceptance of low wages resulted in riots, and many California Chinese were killed. Fear and animosity grew steadily as the various labor groups formed and began lobbying against the hiring of Chinese laborers. In 1879, the California legislature passed a state constitution that prohibited Chinese from owning land, and the U.S. government passed the Chinese Exclusion Bill, which restricted Chinese immigration.

The Chinese Exclusion Bill was the first successful attempt to restrict immigration of any ethnic group, and it probably passed because the Chinese were so very different in appearance, language, culture, and religion from other Americans. In 1882 another Chinese Exclusion Act was passed, which specifically forbade the importation of Chinese laborers and denied American citizenship to American-born Chinese.

Discrimination against Chinese and other Asians continued to be a policy of the United States government and was the first step in a series of attempts to regulate the kinds of immigrants who were admitted to America.

The Chinese were not the only ones who faced increasing discrimination by the 1880s. As each new wave of immigrants hit the shores, the newcomers competed for a place in the constantly changing job market. Employers, especially factory owners and managers were happy to employ the new immigrants at even lower wages than the laborers who were currently working in the mill or factory. That was their way of keeping wages down and profits high. Some unions attempted to organize the newly arrived immigrants, whereas others attempted to exclude them. Nevertheless, immigrants continued to compete for jobs, thus creating antagonism between them and some union members.

Immigrants Find
Work Opportunities
Textile mills in towns like Lowell and Lynne, Massachusetts, were started in the 1830s with American-born

workers. Those laborers were replaced by a series of immigrants beginning with the Irish, who were followed by French Canadians, Italians, and later Poles and Greeks. As each new group arrived, the earlier ethnic workers were forced to readjust to lower salaries and harsher conditions or move on to a new kind of work. This pattern continued until immigration was closed. During the depression, after a series of bitter strikes, most mills moved to the South where they could hire cheap black labor.

Textile mills were a constant source of employment for immigrants, while other opportunities opened and closed. Because immigrants tended to come from the same place at the same time and fit into whatever situations were available to them, some occupations came to be associated with a particular immigrant group. For example, farmers in this nation are often descended from northern European stock, the first immigrants to arrive. Farming, however, was almost completely closed to later immigrants so even if they had performed agricultural work in Europe, they had to adapt to new urban occupations.

Some Irish, for instance, found farm work, but most took the construction jobs that were open to them. Later, many Irish, partly because they were city dwellers, became involved in politics and found places in government jobs, civil service, or the fire department and police force. Italians and Greeks who came after the Irish also settled in cities and performed factory work, but many of them later established small businesses such as barber shops, candy stores, and restaurants. Later immigrants from Eastern Europe, many of them Jews from Poland, Russia, and Romania also settled in the cities and worked first in the factories. Many of them later became public school teachers or entered the new profession of social work. Every new group of immigrants took whatever work opportunities were presented to them at the time they entered.

Though they were consistently discriminated against in the job market, many early immigrant groups gained a substantial footing within a generation. Initial distrust disappeared as they became "real Americans" and joined the majority in its suspicion of the next immigrant group. This process continues today as descendants of immigrants from Greece, Italy, and other Eastern European countries resist the influx of Puerto Ricans into the Northeast, and descendants of Chinese, Japanese, and Irish immigrants worry about the number of Hispanics settling in California and the Southwest.

The complete assimilation of ethnic groups into the general American culture was a favorite prediction of early social scientists who saw this country as a "melting pot" where all the children of immigrants would eventually discard their parents' culture and become "Americanized." Recently, the melting pot theory has become less popular because it is apparent that descendants of immigrants are selectively holding on to portions of their culture and embracing their ethnic heritage with pride.

Heavy Immigration
Leads to Quotas
The period between 1880 and 1914 brought a huge increase in immigration, especially from Eastern Europe, because all of the earlier conditions that were causing immigration intensified and spread. Hunger, unemployment, political turmoil, and worker displacement because of technological advances forced workers to undertake the journey. To these conditions was added the religious persecution of Jews in Russia and Poland.

One measure of how desperate the situation was can be seen by these figures: in 1880 nearly half a million people had immigrated to America; in 1910, however, over a million came in just one year.

City life became much more difficult as immigrants crowded into the places where the rents were lowest and slums were created. The tenements where they lived and the factories where they worked were over-crowded, dark, depressing, and usually without heat or toilets. These living conditions bred disease as well as crime, which made other city residents fear the slums where immigrants lived.

Reactions to the dreadful living conditions of immigrants gave rise to a new profession, social work, and reformers such as Jane Addams organized community centers where people could get help assimilating into the culture. Some citizens were deeply moved by reports of immigrant children dying of cold or starvation, and they offered to help, but many Americans were disgusted by the poverty they saw and blamed the immigrants for creating their own problems. Nevertheless, the overriding reason for prejudice against immigrants continued to be competition in the job market.

Conditions for immigrants in the workplace were terrible, and industrial accidents were commonplace. One report of working conditions at the Carnegie steel mills in the 1870s included this description:

> Many worked in intense heat, the din of machinery, and the noise of escaping steam. The congested conditions of most of the plants in Pittsburgh add to the physical discomfort . . . while their ignorance of the language and of modern machinery increases the risk. How many of the Slavs, Lithuanians and Italians are in-

jured in Pittsburgh in one year is unknown. No reliable statistics are compiled. . . . When I mentioned a plant that had a bad reputation to a priest, he said: "Oh, that is the slaughter-house; they kill them there every day."

Eventually laws were passed to regulate working conditions and prevent industrial accidents. Labor leaders and social reformers led the movement to improve working conditions and eliminate some industrial accidents, but in the meantime immigrant workers paid a terrible price. One terrible accident was the fire at the Triangle Shirtwaist Company in New York City in 1911. In that disaster 146 workers, most of them women, were either burned to death or killed when they jumped from the eighth and ninth floors of the factory. According to a newspaper report of the time, the owner had locked the doors to prevent the workers from stealing. The Triangle fire resulted in new safety regulations and inspections.

At the same time reformers were working to get living and working conditions improved, other leaders were trying to place restrictions on immigration. The number of immigrants arriving staggered the imagination of native-born Americans, and newspapers began to predict an America made up of more Italians, Poles, and Jews than northern Europeans. Prejudice against immigrants had always been great, but it became consolidated in the wake of the tremendous influx of people just before World War I.

After World War I began in 1914, the American labor movement achieved more power than ever before and was able to influence American politics. At the same time, big business no longer needed as much unskilled labor as it had when the railroads were being built and

the factories were just starting. As a result, businessmen stopped resisting the curtailment of immigration.

In addition, many Americans felt more prejudice
against "foreigners" than ever before. The violence of
radical labor unions was attributed to foreign influence, and when the war ended in 1918, many Americans wanted to isolate themselves from the rest of the
world, partly because they wanted to avoid becoming
involved in another European conflict.

These feelings and facts combined to influence
Congress to pass laws that restricted immigration by
establishing quotas on the number of immigrants admitted. The first law, passed in 1921, restricted the
number of immigrants to 357,000 a year and set this
number at 3 percent of each nationality residing in the
United States in 1910. In 1924 Congress restricted immigration even further by changing the quota to 2 percent of each nationality and setting the base year as 1890.
This law eliminated even more immigrants from southern and eastern Europe. The United States had essentially closed its doors.

The period between the two world wars was marked
by economic depression, and immigration was severely restricted despite continued complaints about the
unfairness of the quota system. The reasons for want-
ing to leave Europe increased, especially for the Jewish
people, because the German dictator Adolf Hitler was
imposing anti-Semitic laws on all Jews in his country.
As Hitler's oppression heightened, and Germany began to conquer other European countries, American Jews
fought to have quotas lifted. Some exceptions were
made, but many Jews could have been saved from death
in Nazi concentration camps if American immigration
policies had not been so strict.

Immigration continued to be tightly restricted after

World War II. *Newsweek* magazine described the 1950s this way: "We treated the national character like a prized recipe, to be preserved in perpetuity, in its exact ethnic composition." In 1850 about 11 percent of American citizens were born in a foreign country. By 1890 that figure had climbed to 15 percent. Despite the fact that we are living almost twice as long as a century ago, however, the figure was only 5.5 percent in 1960, illustrating the influence of the shutdown of immigration.

Immigration Patterns Change
One of the reasons given for restricting immigration after World War I revolved around old controversies about skilled and unskilled labor. In the technological age that followed World War II the question of whether or not immigrants were skilled workers took on significance as the cold war between Russia and the United States developed and as scientific technology became crucial to the nation's defense. Many countries, including the United States, raced to admit the advanced scientists who had special expertise in rocketry, nuclear physics, and other scientific and technical fields. So much attention was given to attracting the advanced scientific immigrants that there was worldwide concern about the effect of this "brain drain" on other nations.

In the 1960s, after forty years of fairly strict adherence to the quota system, Congress passed legislation that enabled victims of political oppression to seek asylum here and thus relaxed immigration requirements somewhat. An average of half a million immigrants a year came to the United States during the 1970s, and many of them were not from European countries. However, preference continued to be given to skilled workers. For instance, in 1981, a Mexican citizen without technical expertise could expect to wait fifteen years for a visa. For people of other nations that wait might be much longer.

Because of the acceptance of political refugees, escapees from Communist Cuba flooded into Florida, and Vietnamese refugees claimed political asylum, settling mostly in California. While the new immigrants faced the same assimilation and acceptance problems, their smaller numbers did not affect occupational conditions of other workers except in the case of California agriculture where concern over illegal immigration from Mexico became a familiar issue.

In California, Mexican citizens had worked in the fields since the admission of California to the United States. Many Mexicans settled in California, some had been here since the first haciendas and missions were established. Immigration of Mexicans to the United States was basically illegal, but the nationals fit easily into the Mexican American community.

But as American farm workers began to fight for better working conditions, they encountered the old problems of employers using illegal aliens to keep wages low and to maintain inferior working conditions. The conflict intensified as the number of people entering illegally increased in response to poor economic conditions in Mexico. During the early 1980s illegal immigration grew so rapidly that the San Diego *Union* estimated in February 1983 that 1.5 million people had entered the United States from Mexico since January 1980.

Old patterns repeated themselves as most of these illegal immigrants found work on California farms, competing with the lowest-paid Americans. Some leaders such as César Chavez of the United Farm Workers had long objected to the use of Mexican nationals in the fields. Chavez led a series of successful boycotts and strikes to improve the working conditions of farm workers. He believes the use of immigrant labor, legal or illegal, destroys attempts to organize successful labor unions. Partly because of his efforts, the use of legal work crews from Mexico has stopped, but the illegal workers keep pouring in.

Illegal immigrants often live outdoors or crowded six to a room in shacks. The men stand around the shopping malls in the morning, hoping to be hired as day laborers, often for less than minimum wage. Women work in laundries or as servants. In many parts of the Southwest, Mexicans fill low-paying jobs as waiters, bus boys, dishwashers, ditch diggers, and gardeners.

The 1,093-mile Mexican border is the world's longest and least guarded boundary between a rich industrialized nation and a poor, undeveloped one. Mexicans are tempted to cross illegally by the promise of jobs, education, and the opportunity for a better future. Those are exactly the same reasons that lured earlier immigrants to this country, and American workers are concerned about competition, just as earlier native-born workers were.

There is evidence that the number of illegal aliens entering the nation is increasing, partly because the Mexican economy is in a crisis. In the twelve months that ended October 1, 1983, the United States government apprehended 1,078,469 illegal aliens from Mexico. In the next three-month period, another 3,066,696 illegals were caught. If more than 4 million aliens were caught, an enormous number must have entered the country in that period, since only one out of four illegal aliens is apprehended, according to the U.S. Immigration and Naturalization service.

In 1984, a new immigration bill known as the Simpson-Mazzoli Bill, was being debated in Congress. The bill would make it illegal for employers to knowingly hire illegal aliens. It would also grant legal residence status to many illegals who already live in the United States. No matter what the outcome of the bill, however, workers will continue to enter from Mexico and, like immigrants before them, they will take advantage of the opportunities that are presented to them.

Not all recent immigrants have come to the United States illegally. Since the 1970s, many immigrants from Asia have arrived. Koreans have opened fruit stands in New York City, and Vietnamese have opened restaurants in California and the Midwest. Like other ethnic groups before them, they are making a special contribution to the American worker's history.

6

Women in the Work Force

Colonial Life

The women who settled in colonies were hard workers who came with their husbands or parents in search of religious freedom or to escape poverty and debt. A few adventurous women came alone in search of greater opportunities in the New World.

Many colonial women worked only in their homes feeding and caring for their families. But because of the chronic labor shortage in the early colonies and because most goods were manufactured in small shops attached to the master craftsman's home, many more women were actively engaged in business and manufacturing during that period than is commonly supposed. While it was difficult for a woman to get ahead financially, many single women did own land and earn fortunes on their own. There were some women in nearly every colonial trade including blacksmithing, soap making, candle making, and coach making.

One occupation that attracted a great many women was innkeeping. Opportunities abounded in that field because so many new roads were constructed that the demand for small taverns and inns constantly increased. Many other women became shopkeepers, usually in small establishments that sold tobacco, tea, books, or cheese. These shops were not always profitable, but they were one way some women earned money. Several colonial newspapers were published by women, and the first colonial printer was a woman; Mrs. Jose Glover established her press in 1638. It is likely that more women worked outside their homes during the colonial period than in the nineteenth century, when the factory system eliminated small business opportunities.

Some of the first women settlers, especially those who came alone, were indentured servants who paid for their passage with seven years of servitude. Like the black women who were brought to America as slaves, the female bond servants were cruelly misused, sometimes for immoral purposes. In the beginning, any child of an indentured servant remained in bondage for fourteen years, even after the mother was freed. Often such children were the result of rape.

The position of servants was usually the lowest-paid form of labor a woman could obtain. Women servants were expected to work from before dawn till as late as midnight for very little pay. After the decline of indentured labor, immigrants usually filled these jobs. Farm girls sometimes worked on richer farmers' lands until they married, but they were usually sought after as wives and preferred to work on their own land.

Farm wives worked beside their husbands on northern farms where they plowed the fields, fed the animals, and did many other farm chores. They also made their clothing by spinning flax or wool and then weaving the cloth and sewing clothes by hand.

In most of the eastern colonies and later the states, a woman gave her property rights to her husband when she married. While she might sometimes keep the money she earned or inherited, her husband had the right to manage it for her, and if he invested it unwisely or simply spent it all, she could do nothing about the injustice. Even though women actually had a more nearly equal position during the colonial days than they did later, they did not have anything approaching equality. Most could not vote and had no effective political influence, and married women could not run businesses or manage farms even if the land was their personal property. They were not allowed to hold public office or be leaders in the churches. They were generally taught to read and write but could not attend high school or college.

The basic inequality of women was demonstrated when the colonies gained their independence from England. There was no serious consideration of giving equal rights to women, and the few educated women who protested were not taken seriously. The most famous protest from this period came in a letter from Abigail Adams to her husband, John, who would later be the second president of the United States. She wrote: "If particular care and attention is not paid to the ladies, we are determined to foment a rebellion, and will not hold ourselves bound by any laws in which we have no voice or representation."

The Industrial Revolution
The Industrial Revolution had tremendous impact on the lives of women who worked at home because the textile industry was the first place where mechanization took place. The home spinning wheel and loom, once the center of colonial life, were replaced by large factories in Lawrence, Lowell, and other industrial cities. The machine-made cloth rolled out at an incredible rate and soon made homespun look coarse.

While the textile mills lifted a great burden from women, they also reduced the usefulness of the unmarried women who lived in the households of their relatives. Many unattached women chose to go to work in the factories rather than stay with their families and work for nothing. They worked six days a week, fourteen hours a day, for about $2.50 a week.

While young men in New England were becoming

more adventurous, shipping out to sea or moving west in search of richer farmland, the young women found that working in the mills was just about the only opportunity open to them. Since the men were leaving in great numbers, there was a surplus of unmarried women, and they flocked to the mills in the 1820s and stayed through the 1840s and 50s.

Francis Lowell is credited with the idea of hiring Yankee "girls" to work in the mills. They were supervised closely and required to live in boardinghouses provided by the mill management. Widows ran the boardinghouses, watching over the girls, giving them hearty meals, and insisting that they observe curfews, attend church, and keep their reputations spotless. Some girls chafed at the strict supervision, but most accepted it as evidence of the concern of their employers.

No doubt the emphasis on keeping the girls respectable helped employers recruit other farm girls. They lured the young women to the city with promises of money to spend and stories of the delights of urban life, which included lending libraries, public lecture series, night school classes, literary magazines, and other amenities. Journalists portrayed the lives of the workers as almost perfect, and the publicity brought people from all over Europe and America to see the Lowell mills. While far from perfect, the mills did offer workers much better lives than could be hoped for by their contemporaries in Europe, who still constituted one of the most exploited groups of workers in history. In the 1820s, the work at Lowell was fairly easy, though the hours were long. The mill employees worked from sunup to sundown six days a week with time off for two meals. By the 1830s, however, because of financial problems and increased competition, mill owners and managers began to work the girls much harder.

The Lowell mill girls were the first women factory workers in the United States, and they were also the first workers to organize into groups to protest conditions. They staged many strikes during the next thirty years. Then they were replaced by immigrant labor. Most of the Yankee girls went back to their farms and returned to the unpaid position of wife or daughter. Many others moved west into frontier life.

The Irish immigrants who replaced them were also women, but they were paid less in the 1840s than the Yankee girls had earned in the 1820s. In the 1840s, despite twenty years of turmoil and strikes, the average woman worker in Lowell, Massachusetts worked seventy-five hours a week, fourteen hours a day, and earned less than $6.00 a month. Only the very poorest immigrant women sought factory work, but as immigration increased, a steady supply of labor continued, not only to the mills but to other emerging industries as well. Women and children were regularly employed for lower wages than men, and if they complained, they were dismissed immediately. They were the most powerless group of northern workers.

For many women, the traditional responsibilities such as housekeeping and childcare continued despite the need to work for wages. Many women did piecework at home so that they could work and supervise their children at the same time. They collected pieces of cloth or leather from the factory and sewed them at home. Often they had to leave money as a deposit in case of damage. They worked long hours for very small wages. For example, in the 1840s the "lady shoe binders" usually earned $1.25 a week for the tedious work of removing threads or making tiny stitches in leather. Some went blind from the long hours of concentration on the tiny stitches; many developed per-

manent curves in their backs from bending over the
work. These were the workers who first attempted to
form women's unions with names like the Lady Shoe
Binders or the United Tailoresses Society.

Many of the labor unions that were formed in the
late nineteenth and early twentieth centuries ignored or
specifically excluded women. Jobs continued to be separated according to sex and "women's work" continued to be more poorly paid. The Knights of Labor accepted women, however, and thousands joined when
it was at its height.

Factory owners openly admitted that they employed women and children because they were more
docile than men and earned less. The New York labor
bureau report of 1885 states that women who cro-
cheted shawls made 12 to 15 cents a day. An experienced tailoress earned less than $4.00 a week. That same
year, of the 1,322 women studied in a survey of the New
York clothing industry, 27 earned $6.00 a week and 534
earned $1.00 a week.

*Education is the Key
to Professional Work*
While factory workers were struggling to improve
working conditions, more privileged women were
struggling to obtain an education. There were almost
no opportunities in business after the factory system
took hold. Until very recently, most working women
from the middle class found their job choices heavily
weighted in the direction of teaching, often because it
was viewed as something one might do for a few years
before marriage. Married women were not allowed to
teach in most states until a severe teaching shortage
developed during World War II.

The key to professional success was education, and

as long as women were barred from colleges, they had little hope of becoming doctors or lawyers. The first schools that educated girls beyond a very basic level were seminaries for women, such as the Troy Female Seminary, established by Emma Willard in 1821. In 1837 Mt. Holyoke Female Seminary, the first women's college, was founded. Some months earlier, Oberlin College became the first coeducational college, and thus was the first college to admit women. Vassar, Smith, Wellesley, Radcliffe, and Bryn Mawr followed in the next twenty years.

Few women were able to afford a college education, and most teachers had only a few more years of schooling than their pupils. The establishment of these institutions was a beginning, however, and educated female leaders emerged from the early women's colleges. Some of those graduates were among the first Americans to fight for women's rights. Those leaders worked diligently for sixty years before the vote was granted to women in 1920. In the course of the struggle they achieved many gains for working women, both inside and outside the home.

Though it began in the East, the women's movement had its first real successes on the western frontier. The West was the logical place for the equal rights movement to begin, for women on the frontier had a more nearly equal position with men. In 1869, Wyoming was the first state to pass a law giving equal pay to male and female teachers. It was also the first state to give women the vote. Three other western states—Utah, Colorado, and Idaho—all passed women's suffrage laws before 1896.

The women who lived on the frontier worked long hours at very hard tasks. They worked in the fields, helping with the haying and other seasonal tasks. They

*As her family makes camp for the night,
this pioneer woman chops firewood.*

also tended the animals and kept large gardens. They canned or preserved the foods that their families ate, made their own butter and cheese, sewed their own clothes, knitted sweaters and socks, and even made their own quilts and blankets. Women often built furniture, made soap and candles, and wove straw mats for the floors. Frontier women usually learned to shoot and to care for the sick, and many were responsible for educating their children.

Some women homesteaded alone. Free land attracted the poor and adventurous of both sexes and drew them across the Oregon Trail or other westward routes. On the average, there were four men to every woman in this territory, so women were in great demand as wives, but some adventurous and hardy women preferred to homestead alone.

Property laws were more advantageous to women in the West, and women could own and control property. Few western women had the opportunity to earn a fortune, but some of them held part-time jobs running the local post office, helping neighbors with housework or farm chores, and selling butter, eggs, or produce. Other women found work as "hired girls" on larger farms. As the western population increased, others opened shops in town.

By the late 1880s, many women were teachers, but they nearly always earned less than their male counterparts. Sometimes women were hired to teach four months a year, and men taught during the remaining eight. This was the excuse given for the difference in salary, but the real reason was that women's labor was simply not valued as highly as men's.

A New Class of Women Workers
During the 1880s, most women who worked outside the home were poor. Their basic task was to stave off star-

vation, and to some, the idea of a vote seemed less important than safe working conditions and decent wages.

Around 1900 the situation for women workers in the United States began to change. With the invention of the typewriter and the growth of cities, more educated young women entered the business world as secretaries. These women were usually better educated and wealthier than the factory workers, and they wanted to earn their own money; most of them expected to marry after a short while in the business world.

According to the 1900 census, 5 million women in the United States were earning wages. A great many of these women were working in traditional occupations: 325,000 were teachers; 700,000 were paid farm laborers or managers; and 1,800,000 were servants. These occupations had been accepted as typical "women's work" for some time, since they all involved homes and children. However, almost as many women worked in factories, offices, and stores. There were 932,000 women working in factories, a type of work that had been open to women since the 1830s. Significantly, however, 200,000 women now worked in offices and another 100,000 were employed as retail clerks in stores.

As women from the middle class began to work outside the home in greater numbers, more concern was expressed about their working conditions. Many organizations sprang up to aid women workers, and a great deal of legislation was passed to protect them. By 1907, twenty states had laws that limited the hours and working conditions for women and children. While these laws were intended to help women, many of them stayed on the books and eventually hindered women's progress. Laws against lifting heavy weights, for instance, have kept women out of some higher-paying occupations in industry.

During World War I, many women proved their abilities in traditionally male jobs such as operating blast furnaces. Most of these women were fired when the soldiers returned home (a pattern that would be repeated after World War II), but a precedent had been set. After that, more and more women went to work and earned money of their own.

By the time the nineteenth amendment passed in 1920 giving women the right to vote, large numbers of women from the middle class as well as the working class were holding down jobs outside the home. These women worked as secretaries, clerks, teachers, and bank clerks, and they spent much of their money on themselves. Many of them lived at home until they married and then stopped working and devoted themselves to their husbands and children. As always, a few independent women operated businesses or held down jobs all of their lives, but the majority of middle-class women viewed their families as their primary responsibility.

During the 1970s, women began gradually to break down more barriers, particularly in education. They were admitted to many universities. The women encountered subtle restrictions and quotas, but they hung on despite the difficulties they faced. The women's movement, combined with increased occupational and educational opportunity, has liberated women to an extent that pioneer women never imagined, but even today, women have a long way to go before true equality can be achieved.

The Great Depression
The Great Depression affected women as well as men, though most history books still emphasize the plight of homeless men and boys who rode the rails looking for work. "The women starved to death more quietly," one

woman survivor of that period recalls. While men could move around alone and find enough work to keep themselves alive, the wives and children they left behind were not able to travel. Women with dependent children had to stay at home, so accepting jobs in distant cities was out of the question. These women suffered even more than the homeless men.

Women workers also suffered discrimination during this period. Even if they desperately needed the money, most people thought that hiring a woman was unfair to men. "Give a woman a job and you take one away from a man" was a common saying.

Married women could not find jobs, because employers believed that women ought to stay home and take care of their children while their husbands supported the family. They often had to lie and say that they were single to keep their jobs, because their employers and other workers were sure that a married woman's salary was always "second income" and therefore not crucial. But many married women had to work because their husbands could not find employment or had left home to search for work.

Many women missed out on education during the depression because their parents sent only their sons to school. "All that education will be wasted on a girl," people said. "She'll just get married anyway."

Even though the times were tough, women benefited from some legislation under President Roosevelt's New Deal. Equal pay for men and women was a part of the National Recovery Administration Codes in 1933, though the National Recovery Act was later ruled unconstitutional by the Supreme Court. The Walsh-Healy Act of 1936 made paying men and women different wages for the same job illegal for employees on government contracts, and the Fair Labor Standards Act of 1938 also outlawed double-standard wages.

In addition to sponsoring equal rights legislation, Roosevelt appointed the first woman cabinet member, Frances Perkins, who served as secretary of labor. In his concern for women workers, Roosevelt was influenced by his wife, Eleanor Roosevelt. She was a feminist and had campaigned for women's suffrage and the rights of working women.

Women Workers in World War II
If the depression made it unpopular for women to work outside the home, World War II had the opposite effect. As soon as the United States entered the war in 1941, women began to fill the jobs of the more than 16 million men who went to war.

After centuries of believing that women belonged only in the home, the general public now reversed itself. Suddenly women belonged on assembly lines, in shipyards, and in airplane factories. Even the U.S. Department of Labor made an official statement on this subject: "It can hardly be said that any occupation is absolutely unsuitable for the employment of women."

During the war, women were encouraged to see themselves as useful rather than merely pretty. Rosie the Riveter became a symbol of the woman defense worker. She wore overalls and carried a lunch bucket. A popular movie star of the time was Veronica Lake, whose trademark was her long blond hair, which hung over one eye. She cut her hair short to encourage working women to wear hairstyles that would not present a hazard while operating machinery. Hundreds of thousands of women joined the armed services for the first time, and many of them became officers.

Women responded enthusiastically to the call for their labor in both military and civilian jobs and many of them worked forty-five to sixty hours a week. Large numbers of them earned good money and had savings accounts of their own, and that economic independence changed attitudes about work radically. At the beginning of the war, 95 percent of the women war workers said they would quit when the fighting was over, but by the time the war was actually won in 1945, two out of three wanted to continue working. Most of them, however, lost their jobs when the men came home from the war.

Postwar Women
During the 1950s home and marriage were again touted as women's highest goal. Working women were portrayed in movies as ridiculous or unfeminine and pressure was on women to conform to the old expectations.

In the 1950s, women actually lost ground in most of the professions, including teaching. There were fewer women doctors, lawyers, and college professors in the fifties than there had been in the thirties. While concerned women continued to fight for equal rights, they got no support from men, and most other women ignored them. Congresswoman Helen Gahagan Douglas supported a Federal Equal Pay Act in 1945 and again sponsored one in 1948, but both bills were defeated.

In many ways, women's fight for equality in the job market has been similar to the struggle of blacks. Both movements started as a part of the reform movements of the 1800s, but they achieved limited success in opening educational and occupational opportunities. Nevertheless, both groups were consistently kept out of the mainstream labor force and relegated to "unim-

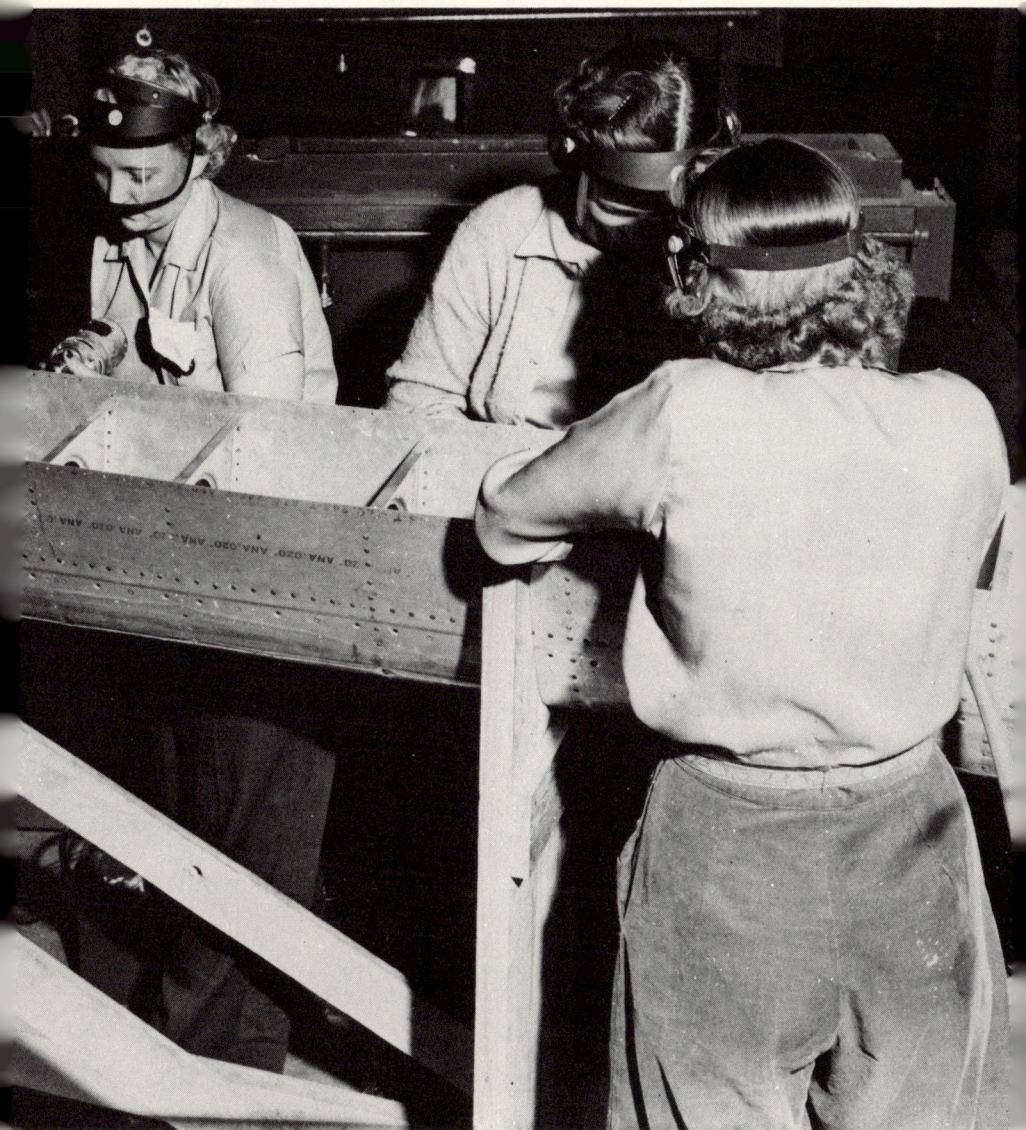

Women hired to work in an airplane factory are trained as riveters before joining the production line.

portant" jobs. Blacks could work as railroad porters but not as engineers. Women could sell merchandise in retail shops, but they were not allowed to sell wholesale goods. Porters earned less than railroad engineers, of course, and retail sales clerks earned less than wholesale representatives. Because the jobs were so different, however, there was no clear-cut way to prove that one group was receiving less money for equal work.

It was legislation designed to help blacks that first gave women a boost toward equal employment opportunities. Civil rights legislation passed in 1964 included a prohibition against sex discrimination by employers. The word "sex" was originally put in the bill by opponents of the legislation in the hope that it would dissuade Congress from passing the bill. In 1964, there was little serious concern about achieving equality in the workplace for women, and the prospect of women working as carpenters, bricklayers, or longshoremen was a joke. The sex discrimination clause was intended to make the whole civil rights bill seem ridiculous, but the maneuver backfired, and the bill was passed.

The women's movement had lost strength in the years since the passage of the nineteenth amendment in 1920, but it was revitalized in the 1960s as women again began to insist on equality.

The women's movement of the 1970s and 1980s focused on every aspect of women's lives—personal, professional, and political. There were many disputes over various issues, but nearly all women agreed on the importance of equal pay for equal work.

The concept of equal pay seemed to affect a large portion of the population directly. By the seventies, most women could expect to spend thirty years of their lives working outside the home, and they no longer thought of their jobs as just something to do until marriage. Yet working conditions and pay still reflected the old notions about "second income."

Because so many more women were working, most Americans were not aware of how deep the discrimination actually was. The situation was worse than most believed because some highly visible women were earning large salaries. But a comparison of women's and men's average salaries told a startling story. In 1977 the average woman who worked full-time earned $6,000 a year while the average man earned $11,800. When broken down by professions, the pattern remained the same; men earned more than women in every occupation except that of kindergarten teacher. Women, in fact, earned 59 cents for every dollar a man earned.

Comparison of men's and women's wages was complicated by the fact that occupations had traditionally been divided between the two sexes. For example, even in the early days, women mill workers received $2.50 a week for tending the looms while men received $10.00 a week for doing mechanical work. The wages and jobs had been separate and unequal ever since. Working conditions for women improved in the late nineteenth and early twentieth centuries, but legal restrictions were placed on the types of jobs women could do in the factory. Those limits made it easier to exclude them from heavier work. Payment was based on how heavy the work was, so women workers who tied wires earned much less than men who lifted tires.

Distinctions between jobs make the issue of equal pay for equal work complicated, and sometimes it has been hard to prove that jobs are on parity. A female secretary, for example, needs language skills, typing, and shorthand, yet she earns less than the male janitor who only needs to know how to use a vacuum cleaner. The secretary may resent her lower salary, but she will have trouble proving that she actually does equal work.

Labor that is traditionally male and neither professional, clerical, nor managerial is often referred to as blue-collar work. Because of the success of labor unions in organizing these occupational groups, many male blue-collar workers earn more than women who are confined to typically female jobs, or "pink-collar" work. As women have pushed for equal pay, many have also pushed for entry into higher paying blue-collar jobs.

Despite their efforts, however, the large majority of women are still in traditionally female occupations. In 1977, seventeen out of twenty women in the United States were employed in clerical, farm, factory, or retail sales positions. The other 12 percent were primarily in "women's professions" such as nursing, teaching, social work, and library science—all jobs that pay less than the "men's professions."

Patterns of sex discrimination were even more apparent in supervisory positions. Until very recently, most businesses and institutions simply did not promote women. Lawsuits instituted in the 1970s and 1980s have eliminated some of these policies, but women still hold very few managerial positions.

Legal actions taken by groups of women, called class action suits, have forced some employers to pay back wages to women who have been discriminated against. Patterns of discrimination are gradually being broken down, and more women work in traditionally male occupations today than at any time in the past. Companies that have government contracts, for example, risk losing their contracts if they discriminate against women. Slowly, blue-collar occupations such as automobile assembly-line worker, railroad attendant, and telephone repair person have become available to women.

There are now female carpenters, roofers, automobile mechanics, and airplane pilots, and women now work in just about any occupation you can think of, but they are a very small minority. U.S. Labor Department statistics show that in 1975 the number of female workers in these jobs was only about 12 percent—only 3 percent higher than the figure for 1960.

Exclusion of women from the blue-collar work force is defended on the basis that women are weaker or that they will have to hear "rough language." The weakness argument is seldom valid, and the "rough language" argument is ridiculous. Neither can be used as a legal excuse to refuse to hire a woman. Meanwhile women continue to fight for the right to hold down higher paying jobs. One woman who used to work in the office of an automobile plant for $5.00 an hour is now working on the assembly line for $7.00 an hour. "Both jobs are boring," she claims, "but I'm a lot less bored when I pick up my paycheck and find almost a hundred dollars a week more in it."

About 52 percent of the women in the United States were working outside the home in 1981. Of that work force, over half were married and most of the others were widowed or divorced. Marriage is no longer an alternative to a career, and today's women know that they must attain equal rights because they will be working most of their lives.

7

The Worker in
Postwar America

Automation Increases

By 1941, when the United States entered World War II, American industry was highly automated. Factories were large, workers were organized into unions, and manufacturing procedures were almost completely dependent on the standardized parts and assembly-line methods developed in the preceding hundred years. No nation on earth was better equipped to mobilize its industrial capabilities to produce the supplies, equipment, arms, airplanes, ships, and motor vehicles that were needed for war.

Workers threw themselves wholeheartedly into the race to build factories. The need for fast production methods spurred the development of new procedures. Some industries expanded almost magically. In 1939, only 50,000 workers were building airplanes, but by 1943, over 2 million people were working in airplane factories, producing 95,000 planes a year.

The war effort became the overriding concern of workers, and movies, posters, songs, and slogans all reinforced the importance of supporting the soldiers, sailors, airmen, and marines who were fighting overseas. Some men obtained deferments from the draft because they were working in vital industry, but many went to war. In their absence, more than half the workers in defense plants were women and blacks who found that they suddenly could get jobs.

During World War II, American industry built 12,000 ships, 300,000 planes, and 87,000 tanks. This tremendous output not only helped win the war faster but also saved many American lives. The advanced industrial capability on the home front gave American soldiers the very best equipment to fight with, making them much better protected than the other armed forces. No country lost as few men in actual combat as we did. Americans turned out more weapons, bombs, planes, and ships than all of the other Allies put together.

Conditions for the average worker were permanently improved during World War II, and techniques for production were so greatly improved that more was achieved in those four years than in the preceding forty. Men and women worked three shifts, and plants were open twenty-four hours a day, six days a week; many workers earned time-and-a-half pay for overtime work. One measure of the tremendous industrial progress made during the all-out effort for wartime production is that a liberty ship took nearly a year to build in 1941 but could be completed in fifty-six days by 1943.

After a decade of depression and unemployment, workers rejoiced at receiving large paychecks every week, often including overtime pay. Many workers saved money because they were earning more, but the war shortages offered them fewer goods to spend their money on. Since most products being manufactured were for the war effort, there were no new cars, houses, or small appliances to buy. There were also shortages of leather goods, nylon stockings, cigarettes, sugar, and meat as well as other items. For the first time, the average American worker had a surplus of money to invest in savings bonds, bank accounts, or other ways.

More opportunities and surplus money weren't the only benefits that workers enjoyed during the war years. Since more people were working, more citizens received Social Security protection and unemployment insurance as well as some protection against discrimination based on race and sex that had been instituted by Roosevelt's New Deal legislation.

World War II marked a turning point for American workers. From that time forward, the emergency measures instituted by Roosevelt during the depression became normal guarantees, and American workers accepted them as a birthright.

Workers Continue to
Prosper After War
The new affluence of workers did not end after the war, but there was sporadic unemployment, and many women and blacks were pushed out of their higher-paying jobs. For the most part, however, the U.S. worker continued to be the highest-paid in the world, and the 1950s and 1960s brought continued expansion with only a few periods of recession.

The production improvements during the war were immediately applied to peacetime industries as research and development done during World War II stimulated new inventions for peacetime use. Radar, which had been used to seek out enemy ships, was soon used to fly commercial airplanes safely at night and to help fishermen predict weather conditions at sea. Other developments in airplane manufacturing were immediately applied to commercial planes, and flying became a common means of transportation.

One invention, the transistor, brought about a revolution in two new devices that had been invented before World War II—the computer and television. Transistors are small electronic devices that replaced bulky vacuum tubes and made portable radios, home computers, and small television sets possible.

Whole industries grew out of this new invention. While large computers, which were basically data-comparison systems, had been in use since the 1880s, the first modern computers with high-speed capabilities came into existence during World War II. These early computers were huge, and only about three hundred of them existed in 1955. After the invention of the transistor, however, computers became convenient to use. By 1980, most businesses were using them for record-keeping, and many executives carried small computers on airplane flights. Thousands of workers were involved in manufacturing, programming, repairing, or operating computers, and computer literacy was required for graduation in many high schools.

Union Membership Slacks off
The gains labor unions made during World War II were somewhat diffused by the Taft-Hartley Act of 1947, which seriously diminished union power. However, labor unions continued to wield great political power in the following decades. Union membership reached 18 million in the 1950s, and one out of three non–farm workers belonged to a labor union. With such large numbers, the strength of the unions and their right to collective bargaining was unquestioned.

After the consolidation of the AFL–CIO in 1955, discrimination against blacks and women gradually diminished, and the union campaigned to enroll service and clerical workers and teachers. Unions made especially good headway in enrolling teachers in the 1960s and 1970s, as teachers' strikes brought higher wages to these historically underpaid professionals.

Despite the attempts of the unions to widen their membership base, union membership began to decrease in the 1960s because blue-collar jobs, which were traditionally the basis of union strength, were declining in number. The process of replacing workers with machines had begun in the 1830s and increased drastically after World War II. The need for semiskilled and unskilled workers declined steadily. Though American workers were better off than they'd ever been before, many were worried about their future.

Old and New Problems for Workers
Two familiar problems—technological improvements and competition from cheaper labor—again began to plague industrial workers after World War II. Business was expanding, and most workers were more prosperous than ever before, but automated devices were replacing workers with threatening speed. Although unions were stronger and workers were protected by contracts and by employment insurance, some occupations almost disappeared between 1940 and 1980.

Dock workers, called longshoremen, had been an important occupational group since the first colonists settled here in the seventeenth century. After World War II, new automated cranes and conveyor belts combined with the growth of air freight to cut down on the need for longshoremen to unload ships. Their strong union was able to limit the number of new members who would be admitted, eliminating some of the possible competition. Soon, only the sons and sons-in-law of longshoremen could get into the union; job security was the big negotiating issue. The occupation gradually closed to younger men, and longshoring became an extreme example of job attrition.

Semiskilled occupations suffered the most because of automation, but technological progress occurred so fast that every American workplace saw a dramatic drop

In many industries, such as automobile manufacturing, robots are fast replacing human workers on the assembly line.

in the demand for unskilled workers. Power machines replaced single-needle sewing machines in the garment industry, and thousands of seamstresses were put out of work. Nylon and polyester clothing eliminated the need for dry cleaning or ironing, and thousands more had to search for other jobs. Even in such traditionally low-paying jobs as fruit picking, laborers were put out of work by automated devices that used iron claws to pick the fruit.

Hundreds of devices were invented to speed up assembly lines. The large overhead cranes that had hauled airplane wings during the war were soon carrying automobile parts in the same manner. Painting that was once done by hand was now done by spray gun; body parts that were once cut individually were being stamped out by large presses; steel parts that had been fastened together by hand with wrenches were now secured faster and better by machine-driven tools.

Because business was booming and industry was expanding, workers who were laid off in one place often found work somewhere else. Union contracts concentrated on fair lay-off procedures and instituted a series of steps leading to seniority status in order to make bumping within a factory more equitable. Under this system, if a worker with seven years on one job was laid off because the job was eliminated, that person could often obtain a transfer to another department, sometimes bumping another worker with less seniority out of a job. Above all, American labor leaders intended to avoid the abuses that nineteenth-century workers endured as they were replaced by machines. Pockets of unemployment inevitably developed, however, and young people looking for blue-collar employment often had trouble finding their first jobs.

Younger Workers Suffer
in Decreasing Job Market

Unemployment never reached anything like the 25 percent that occurred during the Great Depression, but as older workers left, they were replaced by machines. Often the company encouraged early retirement, paying bonuses to workers who chose to leave at age fifty or fifty-five. Some companies simply did not replace workers who left (called silent firing); these policies had much greater impact on young people looking for jobs than on actual employees of the company.

During the 1970s, it became apparent that the United States was facing a new kind of unemployment that affected young workers with no special skills. Unemployment figures were misleading for these unskilled young people, who were simply not qualified for the jobs that were available. There might be labor shortages in certain skilled areas, but the large groups of unemployed workers could not fill those openings.

Automation created special problems for unskilled workers, and the federal government made some attempts to train these unemployed workers for new jobs operating electronic devices, computers, or other technically advanced equipment, but the young people needed a great deal more help than most programs offered, and so the problems were not solved.

Many of these unemployed young workers were members of minority groups. Black teens, who had suffered from a pattern of historical discrimination, including unequal educational opportunities, were severely affected. Among this group the unemployment figure was sometimes as high as 40 percent. It is ironic that while blacks and women were making their greatest strides in opening equal opportunities at work, the actual need for higher-paid blue-collar work was diminishing, and many young black men lost out completely. Because women were usually able to find clerical positions, they suffered less unemployment, but they continued to earn less than men.

The unemployment problem increased as foreign manufacturing strengthened and more assembly work was done outside the United States. By 1980, it was common for manufactured goods sold in the United States to have been produced in Asian or Latin American countries where labor was cheaper. Choices between high wages and full employment sometimes confronted American workers who faced the same competition from laborers in foreign countries that their ancestors had from immigrant labor.

Technology Improves
the Workers' Situation
Despite the fact that technological advances created unemployment for some workers, the automated devices actually improved conditions in manufacturing for most laborers. Industrial accidents that had been commonplace in the nineteenth century were almost unheard of in the twentieth. The use of complex machines, called robots, to replace human functions in dangerous situations eliminated many of the most dangerous jobs. For example, simple robots are now used to pick up red-hot pins in steel plants, work that would be excessively dangerous for a human being. Robots also handle many dangerous chemicals. Workers themselves are protected by electronic sensing devices that alert them to dangerous conditions within a plant.

Worker safety regulations continued to be improved, and the number of industrial accidents declined dramatically in the decades after World War II.

The health and safety of average workers improved steadily, and their average life expectancy climbed from 35.5 years in 1790 to 70.5 years in 1965.

Part of the reason that worker safety improved so dramatically was that fewer people were actually performing labor. Since the 1950s there had been a general decrease in the number of people working on the assembly lines and an increase in the number employed in offices, small businesses, and government jobs. Also, by the 1950s more Americans were employed in service occupations than in agricultural or industrial jobs.

In 1970, more Americans were employed in business and professional services than in manufacturing. While all jobs had increased in number, the difference between the advances in blue-collar and white-collar jobs was striking. Blue-collar jobs increased by only 17 percent from 1952 to 1970, while white-collar jobs increased by 70 percent. A new sort of revolution was taking place.

The Affluent Worker
In 1800, about 95 percent of the workers in America had made their living from agriculture. By 1980, only 5 percent of the country's labor force was needed to feed the nation and produce surplus for other countries. The technological revolution, combined with the inventions of the Industrial Revolution, resulted in more abundant food, shorter working hours, and better conditions for the workers of this nation than their forefathers could have imagined.

American workers had reached their highest level of attainment by the 1980s and were confidently looking forward to the future. Though problems remained and challenges abounded, the average worker had never been better off.

Job security measures started in the 1930s by the Roosevelt administration had been expanded in ways that few could have imagined during the Great Depression. Unemployment insurance, workmen's compensation, and union contracts that included equitable procedures for layoffs and early retirement were just a few of the gains. Child labor was a thing of the past, and women and minorities were holding more and more high-paying jobs.

The lines between the working class and the middle class in America were blurring because the laborers were now as affluent as some of the employers had been in earlier times. American workers owned their own homes, drove their own cars, and sent their children to college. Some were even capitalists with investments in big business. Many workers acquired shares of stock in the companies they worked for through profit-sharing schemes and other investment plans. In 1984, about 18 percent of all Americans were stockholders in some profit-making company. The struggles of their ancestors for a better life had been won to a great extent, and American workers were confident about the future.

8 | Working in the Future

The Challenges Are Great

Most attempts to predict the future are based on the assumption that it will follow the patterns set during the present and past. If we look at the current challenges, we see that one important issue is the continuing struggle of women and minorities for equal opportunity in the workplace. Women and blacks still earn less than white males do. Some social scientists say that women are actually earning 55 percent in the 1980s instead of the 59 percent they achieved during the 1970s. Blacks and women have made some significant gains in visible management jobs, and most companies are careful to have some women and minority members in their work force, but the overwhelming majority of them are in low-paying dead-end jobs. However, women and blacks are clearly committed to becoming full members of the work force, and it is safe to predict that the struggle for equality will continue.

If women workers are to make significant gains, more consideration must be given to the way offices, department stores, schools, and factories are organized. More sharing of jobs between two part-time workers is expected, and plants will probably include child-care facilities. The issue of child care is central to the equal employment opportunities for women, who still bear the primary responsibility for raising children.

One frequent prediction is that as our offices become more and more computerized, people will work in their homes on their own computer terminals, relaying their work to the central office. Whether workers will adapt to the isolation of working at home is ques-

Young people, and especially minority youth,
are especially hard hit by unemployment
in the 1980s. These people are filling out
applications for jobs in a new hotel that offers
the prospect of employment for 1,000 workers.

tioned by other futurists who talk about "beehiving"—the tendency of human beings to flock together. However, many women who are faced with difficult choices between the needs of their children and the demands of their careers may prefer to work at home.

If minority workers are to continue making advances in the workplace, attention will have to be paid to equalizing educational opportunities for them. If steps are not taken quickly to help the less-educated and poorest-prepared youth, a class of unemployable Americans will become a permanent national problem. There is some evidence that a hard-core poverty class has already developed because of the shortage of unskilled jobs, inequality of education, and lack of opportunity for young members of minority groups. A disturbing statistic shows a steady rise in the median income since the 1950s for most Americans, but it also demonstrates that the bottom 20 percent have actually lost ground. Many futurists fear that we are developing a more rigidly fixed class system, with steadily decreasing opportunities for those on the bottom of the economic ladder.

While many of the poorest Americans are older people who live on Social Security or other small fixed incomes, some of the hard-core poor are potential workers. The Bureau of Labor Statistics estimated in 1980 that 24 million people in the United States would take jobs if they could find them. Many of these people are currently receiving government aid; they are unskilled, and many are poorly educated or handicapped. Some are young mothers who depend on welfare for money to live.

Unemployment caused by technical advances will continue to be a problem in a society that is changing as quickly as this one is. New methods of production eliminate more jobs every day. Many occupations have disappeared entirely, and others will also vanish. Soon the need for stenographers, keyboard operators, and typesetters will be eliminated as computers take over their jobs.

Job retraining for workers who are replaced by new technology will become more and more important. Unskilled workers have suffered the most in the past, but clerical workers will soon feel the same threats as computers take over bookkeeping, grocery checking, and secretarial tasks. A major part of union negotiations during the next few decades will center on retraining opportunities, lay-off procedures, early retirement benefits, and seniority rights.

Baby Boom Bulge
The influx of young workers in the 1970s was a result of the high birth rate right after World War II. Those children of the baby boom had become adults and were demanding their place in the working world at a time when jobs were disappearing. Even skilled and college-trained young adults experienced intense competition for positions.

It was not uncommon for a taxi driver to have a college degree in philosophy or for a secretary to hold a degree in English. Those with liberal arts degrees had only a general education and were not trained for any technological specialty; as a result, they were the hardest hit. In occupations such as publishing, sales, law, social work, and teaching, these young people found that there were far too many other baby boomers waiting to fill the slots left vacant by retiring older people. In 1984, a fifty-one-year-old worker born in 1933 was a member of the smallest population age group. The worker who was fifteen years younger was born in 1948 and was a member of the largest population group. It is safe to predict that ambitious baby boomers will be talking about the joys of early retirement to their bosses who are fifteen and twenty years older.

By 1980 young people born in the decade after World War II made up half the labor force instead of the quarter that could normally be expected. While business expanded rapidly in that period, it could not absorb all of the youngest group of workers. Predictably, the job shortage was greatest in the unskilled occupations that were being hard hit by automation, technical advances, and foreign competition.

The United States has been committed to full employment since Roosevelt's New Deal policies during the depression, and several remedies for unemployment among young people have been propounded. They include direct aid to workers by providing government jobs, job training, and retraining programs; increased government spending; and easier credit for businesses in order to create the estimated 20 million new jobs that are needed.

While many young people were struggling to get a foothold on the occupational ladder, there was a shortage of some kinds of laborers. One reason for the unemployment problem is that many American workers are reluctant to take jobs that they perceive as unrewarding or "beneath" them. The gains of earlier decades have created high expectations for American workers, and many native-born Americans are unwilling to work for the minimum wage, especially in positions they consider demeaning, such as cleaning or janitorial work. Jobs that don't pay well or are particularly arduous—such as dishwashing, bussing tables in

restaurants, washing cars, and working in the fields—
are being filled by immigrants from Mexico and Gua-
temala who enter the country illegally.

Immigration Continues
Despite Restrictions
Immigration, both legal and illegal, from Spanish-
speaking countries is increasing rapidly, and predictions are that the influx will continue. What's more,
these Hispanic immigrants have a higher birth rate than
native-born Americans. This means that the Hispanic
population will probably increase dramatically in the
next decade even if the attempts to curtail illegal immigration are successful.

If the Hispanic population grows as rapidly as expected, there will be a number of employment opportunities for bilingual professional and service workers.
Schools, hospitals, grocery stores, police, and social
workers all will need more bilingual workers, and
throughout Florida and the Southwest speaking Spanish will become an important job skill.

A Worker's Life
In the 1800s the average woman lived to be forty-seven
years old. She could expect to marry, bear children, and
if she did not die in childbirth, live to see her first few
grandchildren. Her work was in the home, and the
family revolved around her.

Today, the average woman lives into her seventies,
and young women can look forward to a healthy life
span of perhaps one hundred years. Most women are
having one or two children, but about half of today's
marriages end in divorce. Young women can expect to
work outside the home for most of their lives. Because
of the increased life expectancy and the dramatic health

improvements, they may choose to work into their seventies or eighties.

Men's lives have also changed dramatically and will continue to do so. Those who live past sixty-five today often continue to live into their eighties, and they may choose to ignore the traditional retirement age as well. Because people are living longer, many will also work longer, and many others will continue working part-time. Mandatory retirement age is now seventy instead of sixty-five, and while some workers choose earlier retirement, many others plan to work as long as they can. Part of the reason people want to work longer is that studies on good health in old age prove that active involvement helps keep people young.

The increased interest in working through later years and the presence of women in the work force will stimulate the number of opportunities for part-time work. Two or more people sharing a job, for half of each day, is becoming a common practice. Another part-time work pattern that especially appeals to older workers who want to travel is for two workers to trade six months on and six months off the job.

Change Will Be Normal
Just as a worker can expect to work longer, so he or she can expect to work in more places. We have become a mobile society because of the technological revolution. Not only have automobiles, airplanes, trucks, and trains made it easier for us to move from one part of the country to the other, but many companies have expanded all over the nation and routinely rotate their employees among various branches. Some large corporations are trying to cut down on the number of these transfers, because moving causes family stress and is expensive. At the same time, ambitious workers are

moving more quickly from one job to another, so the moving trend will probably continue or increase. Today, the average person moves every three years.

Conditions will change so much that experts are predicting that young workers entering today's work force will make at least three complete changes of career in their lifetimes. Since automation is rapidly advancing, it is logical to suppose that new jobs will be created that we cannot even imagine today. Could a worker in 1884 have imagined the need for a television repairman? Or a word processor operator? Or a motion picture sound technician?

It is safe to predict that there will be more occupations in the field of computer programming and operating. The computer is revolutionizing office work, and most experts believe that we will soon be working in a paperless work space where all information will be stored and transmitted electronically. Books and newspapers will be written on discs and read from the computer screen.

Computers are a growing area of technology, but they will not provide the greatest number of jobs in the next decades. Most of the future jobs will be in services such as schools, cleaning plants, laundries, restaurants, child-care centers, and gasoline stations. Hospital work—particularly the care of the elderly, because of the longer life span—is one of the fastest-growing occupations. When the baby boomers grow old, it will be an even bigger field. Right now, the baby boom generation is producing a critical need for child-care facilities and schools.

Medical technology has advanced rapidly in the last decade, and devices such as pacemakers to boost a deficient heart will continue to be invented. Jobs in the medical field will change and expand rapidly, and so any health-care occupation is a good bet for the beginning worker.

The need for pre-school child-care facilities may level off within the decade, but the demand for elementary and high schools will continue. The bulge will hit the colleges in about fifteen years, and there will be a demand for instructors, office workers, and building personnel in all colleges. Opportunities in the writing, producing, and publishing of school materials for these youngsters will open up as well.

Because people are living longer and will enjoy longer and healthier retirement years, occupations that relate to leisure activities will continue to increase in importance. The sudden interest in sports and fitness in the United States has given rise to increased job opportunities, from manufacturing jogging suits to managing fitness centers.

Manufacturing will continue to decline in importance in the United States, and some experts predict that the country will be filled with managers who employ workers in other parts of the world. The use of cheap immigrant labor helped to change America from an agricultural to an industrial society. In today's change from an industrial nation to a postindustrial nation, we will probably employ workers in their home countries.

This trend is already in effect in many industries. Television sets put together in the United States often use parts manufactured in Korea or Japan. Automobile factories in Mexican border towns such as Tijuana may be the beginning of a trend that will take hold in the next decade. The Ford Motor Company and others are designing and testing cars here, then shipping the parts across the border to be assembled in Mexico where labor is cheaper. The automobiles are then shipped back to the United States for sale.

The use of foreign labor appears to be growing, although labor unions protest the practice. It is difficult to predict whether the trend will decrease because of union objections or whether it will signal a crucial change in the life of the worker.

Some pessimists point out that the United States is caught in a knot of problems that affect the whole world. The possibility of nuclear war, energy depletion, and overpopulation will affect the quality of life of the worker.

The days when oppressed people could escape their problems by sailing across the sea to freedom is gone. Though it is clear that worldwide problems affect us, the situation is not hopeless. Although futurists fear that we are coming to the end of our energy resources, we are learning new ways to use the sun's rays.

While some worry about the population increase, we see tremendous advances in agricultural technology to produce more food, and there has been a decline of the birth rate in developed countries.

Despite the challenges, there is no reason to believe we are doomed to a future of darkness. The changes that have come so far in the life of the American worker have included more good than bad, and it is possible that the trend will continue.

Some futurists, such as Isaac Asimov, scientist and writer, have optimistic predictions about what is coming next. The automated world we are entering can make work easier, better, and more effective. It can make the quality of life better for the American worker and for workers all over the world. Says Asimov, "This much I know: it will be as far advanced beyond ourselves as we are beyond the Middle Ages."

Index

Italicized page numbers indicate photographs.

Agrarian society, 14
Agricultural Adjustment Act (1938), 53
Agriculture: colonial, 3–6, 7–9, 12, 38–39, 78; 19th century, 18, 20, 40, 42, 48–50, 64, 68, 83–85, 105; 20th century, 52–53, 74–75, 102, 105, 116
American Federation of Labor (AFL), 29–36, 50–51, 65
American Federation of Labor-Congress of Industrial Workers (AFL-CIO), 36, 55, 99
American Revolution, 11, 13, 14, 24, 37, 38, 58
Apprentices, 12, 14, 15, 24
Automation: postwar increases in, 100–103, 109–110, 114, 116; World War II, 96–99. *See also* Factory system; Mass production
Automobile industry, 23, *101*, 115

Baby boom, 110–112, 114
Black Codes, 37–38
Black labor, 37–56, 90, 92; colonial, 6–7, 37–39; and discrimination, 47, 50–51, 53–55, 103; 19th century, 44–50; 20th century, 51–56, 98, 99, 103–104, 106, 107, 109; slavery, 6, 37–44; and unions, 50–51, 55–56

Blue-collar jobs, 94–95, 100, 104, 105
Bound labor, 6–7

Canals, 20, 21, 60, 61, *63*
Carpentry, 7, 8, 12, 24
Chavez, César, 74–75
Child labor, 106; colonial, 8–9; 19th century, 17, *19*, 26, 38, 81; 20th century, 35, 86
Chinese immigration, 65–67
Civil rights, 54–56, 92
Civil War, 22, 25, 37, 48
Collective bargaining, 32–33
Colonial labor, 3–13, 24; black, 6–7, 37–39; female, 9, 77–79; immigrant, 57–58
Computers, 98, 99, 103, 107, 114
Congress of Industrial Workers (CIO), 34–36
Convict labor, 6–7
Craftsmen, 11–17, 23, 24, 29, 58

Eight-hour workday, 26, 28
England, 6, 7, 13, 14, 57, 58
English immigrants, 57, 58, 62
Erie Canal, 21, *63*
Explorers, European, 3–4, 37, 57

Factory system, 13; 19th century, 15–19, 23, 25–29, 39, 59–62, 67, 68, 70–71, 79–82; 20th century, 53, 89, *91*, 96–98, 100–104
Fair Employment Practices Act (1964), 55

Fair Labor Standards Act, 34–35, 89

Female labor, 77–95; colonial, 9, 77–79; and discrimination, 81, 82, 85, 88, 90–95; and education, 82–85, 87, 88; 19th century, 61–62, 67–68, 79–86; 20th century, 82, 86–95, 98, 99, 104, 106, 107, 109, 112–113; and women's rights movement, 83, 86–87, 89, 90, 92–95

Fishing, 9–11, 23

Foreign manufacturing, 104, 115–116

Frontier, 18–20, 23, 45–58, 83–85

Fur trade, 18, 20, 45

Future of labor, 107–116

German immigrants, 58–64

Gompers, Samuel, 29, 30

Great Depression, 33–35, 51–53, 87–89, 103

Haciendas, 4–5

Immigrant labor, 57–76; assimilation process, 62–66, 69, 74; colonial, 57–58; and discrimination, 61, 65–72; illegal, 74–76, 112; 19th century, 21, 26, 28, 58–69, 73, 81; 20th century, 31, 51, 69–76, 112, 116; political refugees, 72–74; quota system, 69–73

Indentured servants, 6, 58, 78

Indians, 3–5, 11, 20, 45, 47, 57

Industrial accidents, 18, 22, 70–71, 104–105

Industrial Revolution, 14–23, 40, 42, 64, 79–82, 105; and union growth, 24–26

Industrial Workers of the World (IWW), 31, 50

Irish immigrants, 58, 60–64, 68, 81

Job security, 102, 106

Knights of Labor, 28, 29, 50, 82

Ladies' Garment Workers, 34

Lewis, John L., 33–34

Longshoremen, 100

Lowell mill girls, 79–81

Management, 19th century workers exploited by, 27–28

Manufacturing. See Automation; Factory system; Mass production

Mass production, 15–16, 23, 102

Meany, George, 36, 55

Merchant ships, 9–11

Mexican immigrants, 73–76, 112

Mill towns, 17–18, 60, 61–62, 67–68, 79–81

Molly Maguires, 26

National Labor Union, 26, 50

Native American party, 65

New Deal, 33, 52–53, 88–89, 98

New England: colonial, 8–11; 19th century factory system, 17–18, 19, 61–62, 67–68, 79–82

North: black labor in, 44, 51, 53; Industrial Revolution, 14–18, 19

Oil, 28

Open shops, 32

Plantation system, 5–8, 38–42, 49

Political refugees, 72–74

Poor whites, 7–8

Postwar labor, 98–106

Railroads, 20, 22, 27, 28, 51, 61, 65–66
Railway Labor Act (1926), 32–33
Reconstruction period, 48–49
Reform movement, 70–71
Religion, 5, 60, 61, 69, 72
Retirement, 113, 115
Road construction, 19th century, 20–22, 60, 61
Robots, *101*, 104
Roosevelt, Franklin D., 33, 34, 52, 54, 87–88, 98, 106

Scottish immigrants, 57, 62
Sharecroppers, 49, 52
Shipbuilding, 9
Silent firing, 103
Simpson-Mazzoli bill, 75–76
Skilled labor, 19th century, 14–17, 24, 29
Slavery, 6, 37–44
Social Security, 97, 109
Societies, 24
South: colonial, 5–8, 37–38; 19th century, 14, 22, 39–42, 48–49
Steamboats, 21, 28
Steel, 28, 70–71
Stock, 106
Strikes, labor, 24–28, 31, 32, 35–36
Sylvis, William, 26

Taft-Hartley Act (1947), 36, 99
Teaching, 90, 99
Television, 98
Tenant farming, 49, 52
Textile industry, 15, 31, 42, 60, 61–62, 67–68, 79–81
Trade: colonial, 11, 38; 19th century, 18, 20, 45; slave, 38
Transportation workers, 19th century, 20–22, 60, 61, *63*, 65–66

Triangle Shirtwaist Company fire (1911), 71
Turnouts, 24

Unemployment: 19th century, 25, 58, 64; 20th century, 33–35, 51–53, 55–56, 87–89, 97, 98, 102–104, *108*, 109–112
Unions, labor, 13, 96; and blacks, 50–51, 55–56; history of, 24–36; and immigrants, 65, 67, 75; 20th century, 99–100, 110; and women, 82. *See also specific unions*
United Automobile Workers, 34
United Mine Workers, 33–34
Unskilled labor: 19th century, 15, 29, 31, 48; 20th century, 31, 102, 103, 110
Urban growth, 19th century, 17–18, 23

Violence, labor movement, 26–28, 31
Vote, women's, 83, 86–87, 92

Wages: colonial, 24; 19th century, 15, 22, 28, 59, 66, 68, 79, 81, 82, 83, 85; 20th century, 34–35, 53, 75, 88–89, 92–95, 99, 109
Wages and Hours Law. *See* Fair Labors Standards Act
Wagner Act (1935), 34, 36
War industries, 96–99
Washington, George, 15, 41, 42
Western expansion, 19th century, 18–22, 45–48, 83–85
Whaling industry, 9, 23
White-collar jobs, 105
Whitney, Eli, 16, 42
Women. *See* Female labor
Workday disputes, 26, 28, 35

Working conditions: 19th century, 17–18, *19*, 22, 25–29, 39, 40–41, 59, 60–62, 68, 70–71, 81–82, 93; 20th century, 34–35, 86, 93, 112–113, 114

World War I, 31, 32, 51, 71–72, 87

World War II, 35, *53–54*, 73, 82, 87, 89–90; automation increases due to, 96–99

Young, contemporary labor problems of, 103–104, *108*, 110–112

WITHDRAWN